ATHLETES MAKING MOVES ™

Copyright

Athletes Making Moves

Secure Your Future by Protecting Your Name, Image & Likeness

By

Sivonnia DeBarros, Protector of Athletes™, Founder & CEO of What Are You Sporting About?™

COPYRIGHT © 2021
WHAT ARE YOU SPORTING ABOUT? PUBLISHING
ALL RIGHTS RESERVED

Published by:
What Are You Sporting About?™
A Brand owned by Sivonnia DeBarros & the
SL DeBarros & Associates, LLC

What Are You Sporting About? Publishing

sdebarros@sldebarros.com
prosportlawyer.com
athletesmakingmoves.com

ORDERING INFORMATION

Special discounts are available on quantity purchases by corporations, associations, and others. For details, contact the publisher at the email address below.

Orders by U.S. trade bookstores and wholesalers.

Please contact *What Are You Sporting About?* Publishing: Tel: (708) 234-7298, or visit prosportlawyer.com

STANDARD EDITION
(Hardcover)
978-1-7375774-0-9
(Paperback)
978-1-7375774-1-6

SPECIAL EDITION
(Hardcover)
978-1-7375774-4-7
(Paperback)
978-1-7375774-5-4

Only available in the Standard Edition
(E-Book)
978-1-7375774-2-3
(Audiobook)
978-1-7375774-3-0

Book & Interior Design by: Sivonnia DeBarros

DISCLAIMER

The information provided in this book is for informational purposes only and is not intended to be a source of legal, sports, or financial advice with respect to the material presented. The information and/or documents contained in this book do not constitute legal, therapeutic, or financial advice and should never be used without first consulting with an attorney, therapist, or a financial professional to determine what may be best for your individual needs.

The publisher and the author do not make any guarantee or other promise as to any results that may be obtained from using the content of this book. You should never make any legal, therapeutic, financial investment or other decision without first consulting with your own advisors and conducting your own research and due diligence. To the maximum extent permitted by law, the publisher and the author disclaim all liability in the event any information, commentary, analysis, opinions, advice and/or recommendations contained in this book prove to be inaccurate, incomplete, or unreliable, or result in any losses, legally, financially, or otherwise.

Content contained or made available through this book is not intended to and does not constitute legal advice or investment advice and no attorney-client relationship is formed. The publisher and the author are providing this book and its contents on an "as is" basis. Your use of the information in this book is at your own risk.

DEDICATION

Considering this beautiful and timely new era on Name, Image & Likeness (NIL), I would be remised if I didn't acknowledge and dedicate this book to one of my most favorite, bubbly, sweet, handsome, and sincerest cousins who is truly missed:

JOHNNY "J-RED" ADAMS

Without a doubt, Johnny was an exceptionally talented athlete who excelled at football and track & field. Had Johnny lived and did so with the same opportunity of NIL, I know that he would have taken full advantage.

This book is a toast to you cuz. You may be gone, but you'll never be forgotten.

With much love,
Vonnya.

NIL TOOLS

Before you get deep into this book and start earning from your Name, Image, & Likeness (NIL), I want to make sure that you have a dedicated place to visit for updates, along with standard form templates to help you maximize your opportunities.

As you know, trying to keep a book updated with changing rules and demands around NIL will be challenging, so I have created this **FREE** virtual *Athletes Making Moves Portal* for you.

First, you'd need to register your book at **www.athletesmakingmoves.com/registermybook**.

Second, you'll have the ability to create your account on the portal to unlock the resources located at the end of this book in ready-to-use formats, and gain access to additional bonus content and private invitations to Athlete Masterminds with industry experts.

Once you're inside, send a shoutout to me @athletesmakingmoves and @whatareyousportingabout and say #ImMakingMoves.

See You Soon.

TABLE OF CONTENTS

Athletes Making Moves

Secure Your Future by Protecting Your Name, Image, and Likeness

CHAPTER 1

Lay the Groundwork First, Please Sir/Ma'am

Here it is. The first book dedicated to Name, Image, and Likeness (NIL) issues. It's a hot topic generating much debate, contention and excitement. But let me share something with you, whether you're a college athlete, a pro athlete, or retired athlete, to be able to step into the shoes that will secure your NIL like a boss, you must lay the groundwork for yourself.

I want to take you on a journey to have your own say. To do this in the NIL space or any other, you must understand how to properly implement and **Have Your S.A.E.**™ which is the foundational basis to the keys that will truly unlock the world around you.

Before you freak out on me, let me define what S.A.E.™ is:

1) Shifting Your Mindset for Success
2) Achieving Through Accountability
3) Excelling Through Education

You ready?

Shifting Your Mindset for Success

Let's start with **success**. What does that mean to you?

You can learn a lot about people just by how they answer that question.

When I was younger, I might have said: "Oh, I'll be successful when I have a five-bedroom house, a ton of money in the bank, and a nice luxury vehicle." Haha. I bet you agree with me right now, don't you?

That narrative is true for most people, athletes included. They think that one has only garnered a particular level of success when they've made x-amount of dollars, or when they can purchase a high-ticket item that represents money.

Think about it though... that's such a restrictive and mediocre thought process. Money is only one small variable in the massive ocean of success.

I realized that – for me – success was more than money. Success was having a child that I could love and show the world to; traveling without restrictions; the ability to buy myself, my husband and child what we need and want. Success to me is knowing that I can buy that luxury vehicle but don't **need** to.

Success to me is the ability to walk inside my peaceful home and smile at the beautiful and loving environment we've made for our child to grow up in.

Success for me was the ability to pitch in when our furnace went out during the pandemic, and it cost $8,000.00 to replace after my husband had been laid off for a bit. Success was the ability to buy groceries and pay these bills during the pandemic when others didn't know where their next meal was coming from.

You feel' me?

We've gotten so caught up in trying to tell or show everyone our business that we've forgotten what makes "me" happy on the most foundational and fundamental basis.

Therefore, you must engage in the mind-shifting process around success right NOW so that when it's time for you to monetize, promote, and protect your NIL, you're not out here making moves that are not in line with what you really want and the life you desire to build.

Sivonnia, you ask, "how do I shift"? Well, let's start with going back to my first question on success. Think of what success looks like to you and then list all the things that have influenced you to believe or think that way.

You can also shift your mind around sports and what that means to you. For instance, what is the first word that comes to your mind when I say team? You probably answered with some sort of team name, a sporting event, etc. But team can also symbolize leadership, identify, commitment, ability to follow rules, working with others, selflessness, etc.

You catch my drift, right? There are so many things that have been planted deep down inside of you that have caused you to believe there is only one particular way to think about (or do) things.

Therefore, we must disrupt those beliefs so that we can begin to shift our minds around what truly matters. When we've accomplished that, then we'll begin to see how success fits into the equation and how it factors into our daily living.

Achieving Through Accountability

Let me be real with you. It doesn't matter how many opportunities you receive with NIL, if you aren't accountable to yourself, it will all fade away.

Accountability is something that a lot of people have a hard time dealing with. For example, some of the top – TOP – athletes are not held accountable for much because they have all sorts of people to "fix things" or "do the work" for them. But there will come a time when even those "do-ers" can't solve the problems or do the work because the accountability will fall squarely on the athlete.

Think of it this way. Have you ever heard the phrase, "fake it til' you make it"? I have. I literally cringe at it. I've seen so many kids "fake it til' they made it." I've seen college athletes "fake it til' they made it." I've seen professionals "fake it til' they made it." And guess what... They couldn't sustain themselves and the platform they built because they were so busy faking it the entire way up, that when they made it, their credibility and reputation burned to the ground.

They rose the ranks on an illusory idea of achieving, only to discover that the lack of accountability would take them back to square one.

I remember this basketball athlete from my high school (GHS) in Gainesville, FL. He was so athletically talented. But he did not do his work.

His teachers and everyone around him helped him to pass. I remembered he got an offer from the University of Florida (UF) and a second offer from another large university whose name escapes me.

I believe he attended UF but couldn't keep up academically. Then he went to another school and again couldn't keep up. There was no amount of athletic skill that could save this young man.

I haven't heard from or about this athlete. No-one has seen this dude in years! It's like he's withered away. Sad. He didn't hold himself accountable to all of the work that was required to build and maintain his dream, and his dream dropped right into the garbage can because of it.

Remember JaMarcus Russell who played for Louisiana State University (LSU), a first pick for Oakland Raiders who signed a multi-million deal but lost it? Here's the tea. JaMarcus's coaches didn't believe that he was watching and studying game tapes so they gave him blank tapes. When the coaches later asked JaMarcus what he thought, he gave false statements about certain plays and the coach told him the "tapes were blank." JaMarcus, an instant millionaire, was too lazy to watch tapes. He was seriously faking it relying purely on his raw talent but that wasn't enough without accountability. He only played three seasons.

Whether you're playing at the college level, competing in the pros or retiring from the game, you're going to have to demand self-accountability every step of the way to achieve the things your desire.

There is no "fake it til you make it!" Don't buy into that! That attitude (or belief system) is designed to keep you down and defeated. If you hold yourself accountable, you'll be empowered to hold others around you accountable also. With that, not only will you achieve your goals and dreams, but those who've you empowered will do the same and be better because of it.

Excelling Through Education

I just ended the last section around accountability on this amazing athlete who was never self-accountable. A good part of his failure was rooted in the lack of education. But education isn't just schoolwork. Education is all around us. If you're anything like other athletes, I'll bet you are working hard to change your circumstances, so you can have it better than what your parents had and what they were able to give you. Right?

How you gon' do that if you don't know a damn thing? So many people want to change their circumstances but are not willing to educate themselves to do so. It's impossible to teach what you don't know, and that's why your parents could only give you the bare minimum until they knew better.

To accomplish anything, to shift one's entire mindset, to even hold yourself accountable, begins with education. Education is vast. It opens doors that many would never think possible.

And no... you don't have to be a darn Einstein to be educated. God knows I'm not. Education allows you to think differently, think broader and discard the constricted thoughts and belief systems you've built – or that other constructed - for you.

Never think that being a student is the only way to being educated because it's not. You can become educated by reading articles and magazines on matters that impact you.

You can talk to elders and mentors about different business aspects to gain a greater understanding about what you're doing right or wrong. You can sign up for a four-week course just on branding and marking. It's all education. It's just takes on different forms. Always be willing to educate yourself because with what you learn, you will excel higher than you can imagine.

Now that I've broken down those three pillars, you know what it takes to build and set the groundwork to Have Your S.A.E.™. When I mention "S.A.E." throughout this book, you'll know what I'm talking about.

Keep the following in mind as you finish reading this book:

1. How do I define success?
2. What aspects of my thinking need shifting?
3. Am I holding myself accountable?
4. Are others holding me accountable?
5. Or am I allowing myself and others to keep me down by "faking it."?
6. Am I really achieving?
7. What's the importance of Education to me?
8. Have I taken education seriously?
9. What are some non-traditional ways that I can use to get educated?

Now, as we say in law, let's get ready to dive into the "meat and potatoes."

"It's impossible to teach what you don't know."
~ **Sivonnia DeBarros,** *Protector of Athletes*

PART-I

DEAR STUDENT ATHLETE ENTREPRENEUR

CHAPTER 2

Historical & Future Impact of Pay to Play

In this chapter, I'll focus on the National Collegiate Athletic Association (NCAA) since it's the largest college sports association and most popular among student athletes. Let's talk about the historical aspects of college sports as it relates to *Pay to Play* first.

Historically

Every college athlete has had – at one point or another – to learn about the NCAA's prohibited conduct which could lead to ineligibility. However, such prohibitions may be preempted by state law with the new name, image, and likeness (NIL) legislation popping up all over this country.

Prohibition of things like taking payment, extra benefits, money in exchange for complimentary tickets, loans and promises to sign deals were – and currently if your state does not have NIL legislation - a huge no-no.[1]

9

Here's a great example of one of NCAA's written rules for student-athletes: "You are **not eligible** in a sport if you ever have accepted money, transportation or other benefits from an agent or agreed to have an agent market your athletics ability or reputation in that sport."[2]

This brings me to my next point. Remember Christian Dawkins? Ok, buckle up because this situation sounds like it's straight out of a Lifetime movie.

Christian was a young aspiring sports agent who created a business relationship with a guy that he thought was legit.[3] Turns out, "homeboy" was a damn FBI agent, who's entire job was to get Christian to pay coaches in hopes of creating a federal bribery charge.[4]

Now Christian had many connections in sports. How? I don't know. He's very charismatic so maybe that helped. Christian knew a guy from Adidas who he spoke with often and with whom he cultivated a great relationship.

So, Christian's new business partner, who he called D'Angelo, kept pushing and pushing him to pay college coaches to convince basketball players to come to their schools. D'Angelo basically said that since he was funding the business and Christian's interest in the business, that he wanted him to pay these coaches.[5]

Repeatedly, Christian told him that what D'Angelo was asking him to do didn't make any sense. After consistent demands by D'Angelo, Christian finally agrees. Then, boom! Federal bribery charges and more are dropped on him and others.[6] There were multiple college coaches implicated in the matter but Christian would not give the FBI agents 15 to 20 other names to "cooperate" with them.[7] Frankly, I don't blame him.

In my opinion, the FBI set Christian up to take the fall. Basically entrapment. He told this guy numerous times that his plan did not work. That they could get players better than that because players have relationships with coaches in their communities.

Specifically, Christian stated: "There's no need to pay a college coach because those players are coming to college with agents. The idea that it's an amateur world is not real."[8]

Players, coaches, and executives were caught in the aftermath of this bribery mess. Coaches were fired and kids like Brian Bowen II - a 5-star recruit and potential lottery pick – was left without NCAA eligibility.[9]

Apparently, Brian Bowen II's dad allegedly agreed to accept $100,000.00 from Adidas if he played for Louisville.[10] I don't know where this young man is now in his sporting career, but this situation possibly ruined any chance he had of getting to the NBA.

Under the NCAA's historical rules, those things were prohibited and could possibly land someone in prison. But paying players was not an isolated event.

Look at Reggie Bush for example. Once a former Heisman Trophy winner and professional football player, Reggie was stripped of that title when it was discovered that his parents were put in an expensive home for free while Reggie was a student athlete![11]

If my memory serves me correctly, I think it started when Reggie decided to cheat his former agent by not repaying him all of the money that he provided when Reggie was in college. Reggie went with a different agent and his former agent came back saying (not verbatim), "Hold up... I put your family in a house while you were in college, and no-one paid a dime."

Being greedy and playing dirty with the former agent caused Reggie to lose his college Heisman trophy while playing for University of Southern California (USC). And - get this - Reggie's former alma mater (USC) completely disassociated itself from Reggie.

The point of this story is that Reggie still suffered consequences – as a Professional Football player - by engaging in NCAA prohibited student-athlete conduct at that time. His current status as an NFL baller couldn't save him from NCAA's wrath.

In 1987, Southern Methodist University (SMU) was hit with NCAA's "death penalty" (removal of the football program) when a large scheme of paying players was revealed.[12] During that time, "boosters, regents, players and coaches conspired for the most brazen, widespread pay-for-play scandals in the NCAA's history."[13]

I can go on and on about players being paid to play. There are many current and former coaches who as student athletes back in the day, were also probably paid themselves. But... they were never caught. There are pro athletes now who received money, gifts, loans, cars and more but were never caught.

At the end of the day, paying athletes is something that was going to have to be dealt with eventually. Christian Dawkins said it himself: he would never call student athletes amateurs. I agree. These players are competing at a high level and using their skill to hopefully put them on a path that will promote them to the pros.

It's high-time that NCAA stops punishing these student athletes for receiving payment because of their skill – essentially, their NIL.

Most of these athletes are coming from low-income communities dreaming of an opportunity that can – and will – change their lives. On top of that, many of them are using the resources they **do** receive to care for their families – an issue they shouldn't have to be concerned about right now, but they are.

The Push for National Rules Around NIL

In 2019 (at least that's when my Spidey senses were sparked over student athletes being allowed to get paid) there was a lot of noise being made in California regarding NIL.

At that time, three states led the charge – California, Colorado, and Florida – passing legislation allowing athletes to profit from their NIL. As of publishing this book, more than 20 states have officially passed NIL legislation, around 11 states are set to take full effect in year 2021 and many others have introduced NIL legislation.

In my opinion, it's time. Considering the sharp penalties that have rained down on student athletes for accepting money etc., it is a bit unfair when you think about the agents who approached them and never suffered any professional consequence.

The flip side to that is also thinking about the athlete's mindset around building net worth and taking care of their families.

Now, there is a push more than ever by student athletes, parents, coaches, and legislatures to "let them get paid." I couldn't agree more. Playing at the collegiate level does not necessarily guarantee a star player that he or she will make it to the pros. They can get injured and lose their entire sporting future.

However, allowing student athletes to profit from their NIL will allow student athletes to receive compensation from more relationship deals beside sports. It will allow the student athlete to think about their passions and goals, connect with brands that they have always loved in hopes of promoting them, or simply just by starting their own side business or brand.

Because of this push for students to control their NIL, the NCAA has been pushing for Congressional support.

Precisely, the NCAA is seeking for Congress to implement nationwide legislation allowing it to have antitrust exemptions to layout regulations around name, image, and likeness, instead of having individual federal rules that preempt certain state rules.

Senator Chris Murphy from Connecticut made a great statement in response to the NCAA request, saying that the NCAA has never cared about the students.[14] It has basically put the dollar before the student.

Senator Murphy further argued that the NCAA does not need Congress to give it antitrust rights to do the right thing by allowing these athletes control over their name, image, and likeness.[15] One mic drop he gave us was the following:

> So we need to be really careful to not simply put the fate of athlete endorsement deals in the hands of the

NCAA and its rule makers, who haven't shown much historical interest in putting the interests of kids ahead of the interests of athletic programs.[16]

In July 2020, NCAA provided a proposed draft to Congress of its NIL rules.[17] In that proposal, the NCAA speaks loudly about the following:

A) Protecting itself from litigation by multiple states across the country because of individual state NIL legislations,
B) Setting up "guardrails" to protect gender equity in programs, avoid athlete tax liability, ensure that an employer-employee relationship with athletes are not derived by mere NIL legislations;
C) Barring states from creating or continuing any laws regulating an athlete's compensation, IP rights, employment status, or any benefit from their name, image, or likeness;
D) Protecting itself from "unfair competition statutes" or tortious interference statutes;
E) Determining some rules around joint marketing or commercialization of IP rights owned by the association and/or the athlete;
F) Creating procedures or guidelines to investigate or enforce any violation of rule, standard or procedure.

Although the proposal contains more, the above list proved important because it speaks straight to some of Congress's sentiments which I've previously noted.

However, what student athletes must keep in mind is that the students are not employees of their educational institution or with the NCAA. So what will you do when the NCAA or your school says that they are going to have rules where the student athletes must allow for joint marketing of that student's NIL with their school?

What if the student athlete only wants a small sponsorship deal to build on separately and apart from the school and its athletic association?

Will the student get a "piece of the pie" for that joint marketing deal, or would that be mandatory to promote games and campus events?

It makes me wonder if the NCAA is now saying that it wants full control to determine and scrutinize every student athlete's third-party contractual relationships for some other motive? I wish I knew.

What I do know is that student athletes deserve to control their NIL independent from their school of choice and from the athletic association run by people who are not in the student athletes' shoes or that wouldn't dare ask to "walk a mile" in them.

I will say, however, it does make sense to have national rules around NIL because a lot of legal confusion could result for student athletes who seek to transfer to another school or division for one reason or another. However, it's necessary for the federal government to review the longstanding unbalancing of resources for the majority of athletes who participate in collegiate sports to truly determine how much regulation is necessary and to balance that against the student athletes needs and desires to create and sustain wealth earlier on. This can definitely be a game changer for the student athlete.

At this point, it's unclear whether Congress will enact nationwide rules or give the NCAA the power to enact a widespread rule governing NIL although multiple bills have been introduced around student athlete bill of rights and NIL capabilities. We'll all have to wait and see.

Nonetheless, considering that states have introduced, passed, and enacted NIL legislation, the floodgates have been ripped open.

If other states don't propose NIL legislation, it could mean an unbalanced bargaining power to convince prospective student athletes to come to their school because of the opportunity to profit from their NIL without the turmoil and wrath of the NCAA or any other athletic association somewhere else.

"Progress is impossible without change, and those who cannot change their minds cannot change anything."
~
George Bernard Shaw

CHAPTER 3

It's time to
Have Your S.A.E.™

First, Congratulations are in order! For decades, many have argued in favor of student athletes having rights to their own name, image, and likeness (NIL).

Let's face it; many athletes from brown and black communities viewed their scholarship as a ticket to their future. In large part of this, coupled with amazing and once-in-a-lifetime talent, agents would flock to athletes providing brief and quick relief payouts for a promise to sign with their agency when going pro. As discussed in Chapter 2, this, along with other potential factors, contributed heavily to student athletes losing their eligibility.

The push to allow student athletes the right to profit from their name, image, and likeness was made first by California. However, Florida was supposed to be the first state to make their legislation effective on July 1, 2021 pushing them over California and Colorado for the student athlete's benefit.

Then, out of nowhere, Illinois bow guarded its way on top making their NIL legislation effective on June 29, 2021.

Many knew that California, and then Colorado (both very liberal states) passed legislations with effective NIL start dates around 2023, then Florida came in saying they were going to kick things off on July 1, 2021, and did just that. Along with Florida, Alabama, Georgia, New Mexico, Mississippi, Ohio, and Texas, all enacted their NIL legislation on the same date.

But just knowing that one state or another may have effective NIL rules for student athletes isn't enough. Let's say you're lucky enough to be in that state or are considering a school in that state, how will you leverage this opportunity?

Like many opportunities, this can be fleeting. You're probably thinking, "how can this be fleeting when it's law?" Well, the opportunity to maximize the ability to profit from your NIL can be fleeting if you do not begin to create a mind shift around being a student, an athlete and an entrepreneur.

What many athletes fail to understand – pros included – is that you were in business from the moment someone gave you something of value in exchange for talent! Period! You are, in all intents and purposes, an entrepreneur. But first, you're a student. You attend college because you know that you want to gain an education and have a skillset to maximize later in life. **Then**, you're an athlete.

Yes, being an athlete may be seen as a "way out," but you also love it. You love competing and being the best. You love seeing your name in lights and on your school flyers. And guess what? You've probably thought to yourself, man I wish I could get paid for all that.

If you say I'm lying, then tell me what you **are** thinking, because I remember how the gymnasium bleachers would roar when my cheerleading team would hit the floor.

I remember how the stadium bleachers at the UF would give off thundering sounds when my high-school team competed in the Florida Relays. I remember hearing friends and other college kids yell my name at the University of South Florida (USF) as I came off the curve competing in the 200m sprint. Coupled with all of that, there was always a dream of "Wow, what if this could be my life always."

But one thing student athletes forget to think about is that they are **more** than athletes. As I said, in one breadth, you are a student, an athlete, and an entrepreneur. Now think about all the other things that make you great!

Think about the qualities that set you apart from everyone else – on and off the field, court, track, or pool. Think about your individualized characteristics and your "extra sauce" that you take extra time to add into everything that you do! That's important.

You must carry that with you in this new journey and take every opportunity that presents itself. It does not mean that each opportunity will pay off. What it means is that you are staying in motion – acting on those things that could absolutely change your life!

Let me tell you a quick story. Growing up, I always remember hearing my mom say that she wanted her children to do better than she did. Now, that's a mouthful considering my mom was a UF graduate with honors and raised four-children practically solo.

Other times, I would hear various relatives talk about children choosing a profession where they did not have to work themselves to the bone. For example, becoming an architect versus a construction worker; an engineer versus a mechanic; a lawyer versus a cleaner to name a few.

You probably have never thought about this, but being an athlete is a very hard job. You work tirelessly to perfect your craft – your athletic art. You sacrifice a lot to compete. Trust me, this will not be the only time in life that you make sacrifices. But if you're going to make a sacrifice at least sacrifice for the right reasons.

No, this isn't a "talk you out of being an athlete" book because I honestly believe that being an athlete is a perfectly great characteristic and quality to have.

What I **am** talking about is ensuring that you start thinking holistically about what you want to do with owning your own NIL. Who do you want to do business with? How do you see your NIL being portrayed in this world? What impact do you want to have?

After all, you're a student-athlete entrepreneur and it's imperative that you **Have Your S.A.E.**™ [18] in everything surrounding your NIL. You should have the ability to control how you'd like others to perceive it. You should have the ability to protect all that you create because of it.

As a student athlete, you must think critically about this opportunity sooner rather than later, and plan more aggressively to take advantage of the new laws that are dropping.

These are opportunities that former athletes like me wish they had. The ability to build something amazing, begin to build sustainability for the life you envision in the long run. Essentially, this is a golden ticket being handed to you. But without the proper foundation, this opportunity will be fleeting.

Start utilizing this information and the time granted to you to set up strategies for how you want to maximize the NIL opportunity.

Listen. I want nothing but the best for you, but you must first **want the best for yourself**. You can read this book much as you like, but if you do not begin to think strategically about your life – your future – and how you envision it, you will fall between the cracks. Basically, it's time to put on your big girl – or big boy – pants, be assertive and demand what you need. Of course, with respect.

Now. Get ready for the time of your life because the opportunity you have to create a foundation that can set you on a lifetime trajectory of financial stability and freedom is waiting!

Before we end this chapter, I want you to go to the end of this book in the Student Resources and take the Student Athlete Entrepreneur Audit to see where you are and what you need to do to get prepared to own your NIL like a boss.

You betta work!
And remember, it's time to Have Your S.A.E.™

"If you're searching for that one person that will change your life. Look in the mirror."

~

Kara Goldin

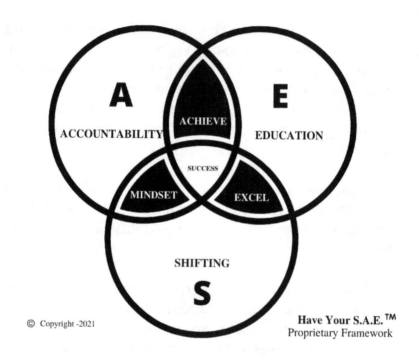

Have Your S.A.E. ™
Proprietary Framework

CHAPTER 4

N.I.L. Legislation: Let's Break It Down

In 2019, everyone was sitting on the edge of their seats as California announced its Bill – *Fair Pay to Play Act*,[19] that will allow college student-athletes to profit from their name, image, and likeness (NIL) and set to take full effect on January 1, 2023.

Florida, out of nowhere, jumps over California, introduces a bill, passes it, and went effective on July 1, 2021 along with other states but did not see Illinois coming as I previously explained.

Since Florida was the first state to make such a bold move, let's talk about its legislation keeping in mind that other states NIL legislation (like Illinois's) may have similar characteristics, but also differ. I know you're probably asking what's in this legislation? How will it be different because athletes have been profiting from their names "under the table" for a long time?

For starters, college athletes would not need to sneak around to engage in under-the-table deals and promises with agents. Generally, the bill allows the student athlete to profit from their NIL, albeit with some exceptions which we will discuss.

Florida's bill focuses on three types of athletes: 1) prospective athletes transitioning to college, 2) Minors at the college level, and 3) adult college athletes.

The Three Student-Athletes

The Prospective Student-Athlete:

Specifically, under Florida's Act, it provides that "A postsecondary educational institution, athletic association, or other group or organization with authority over intercollegiate athletics *may not* provide or offer to provide a *prospective student* who may participate in intercollegiate athletics with compensation in relation to the student's name, image or likeness."[20]

A few things concern me about this provision. First, a prospective student is a student who has not yet become a college student athlete. Second, it's silent as to whether the prospective student can receive compensation from a third-party that is not deemed to have authority over intercollegiate athletics for their name, image, and likeness. Third, it's silent as to who is comprised of the "other group or organization" for purposes of such provision.

Aside from these issues, it appears that the rule is safeguarding against a postsecondary educational institution or athletic association providing payments to prospective students in hopes of inducing that student to accepting a scholarship to attend and compete in athletics at that institution.

That notion speaks to the traditional rules laid out by NCAA whereby it prohibited college athletes – prospective and current – from receiving compensation. Traditionally, a student athlete would lose their playing eligibility if they were found to be in violation of such rules.

The Minor Student-Athlete:

Although it appears that everyone at the collegiate level are considered adults, there may be a chance that your teammate graduated early from high school and are participating in intercollegiate sports at a ripe age of 16 or 17 years old. [21] Heck, maybe you yourself are the minor student athlete.

Under Florida state rules, you are a minor until you have reached the age of 18, unless you have been adjudicated an adult for certain purposes.

Why is this important? If you are a minor signing an endorsement deal, brand affiliation contract, etc., general contractual rules across the country have deemed contracts signed by minors to be void because minors by law, cannot provide informed consent.

Therefore, as a minor student athlete, your guardian would have to sign the agreement on your behalf if you are 1) a resident of the State of Florida, or seeking services to be performed or rendered in the State of Florida; 2) as a minor student athlete you'll be performing or rendering "artistic or creative services or license [your] name, image, or likeness while participating in intercollegiate athletics."[22]

It's necessary to remember that even if you are a minor student athlete who's residency is in another state whereby you would be considered an adult at 17 years old, you would still need the consent of your guardian to enter into performance contracts or deals where you would profit from use of your NIL in Florida.

The Adult Student-Athlete:

Unlike the red tape that minor and prospective athletes must ensure they are not crossing, adult student athletes (the age of majority) are able to immediately consider and dive into certain NIL opportunities.

It's imperative to remember that as you consider certain contractual relationships and deals, that you begin to strategically think of the representation around the deals you will need.

It is one thing to be a student athlete only having to maintain a schedule for practice, class and studying; it's another when you are now an entrepreneur and managing a professional team of individuals and contractual timelines and duties.

There's immense opportunity here, but to take advantage of that opportunity, it's going to take a keen eye for detail, commitment, and accountability to yourself, your brand, your purpose, and the future you want to build.

The Act: What's in It?

Prohibitions:

First, the Act prevents a "postsecondary educational institution" (basically, your school) from engaging in the following:

(1) upholding any rule or requirement that would usurp the student athlete's right from participating in certain intercollegiate athletics that would allow the student athlete to profit from his or her name, image, or likeness;

(2) negatively impacting that student-athletes scholarship eligibility by way of the student-athlete receiving compensation from his or her name, image, or likeness;

(3) preventing the student-athlete from hiring professional representation to advise the student-athlete in matters of contract, legal matters, or sports;

(4) preventing a student-athlete from engaging in a contract for the "student's name, image, and likeness for commercial purposes when the student is not engaged in official team activities;"

(5) preventing the student-athlete from obtaining professional representation.

Second, with regard to athletic associations and conference groups like the NCAA that have control and authority over certain postsecondary educational institutions, the Act states that these types of organizations may not prevent a student athlete from "(1) profiting from his or her name, image, or likeness;" and (2) it may not retaliate against an educational institution in participating in certain intercollegiate athletics just because a student-athlete is profiting from his or her name, image, and likeness.

Third, as for students, aside from the other issues discussed above, you are required to provide disclosure to the school's official regarding your contract for compensation of name, image, likeness.[23] Furthermore, you are prohibited from engaging in any contractual relationships that may be deemed a conflict of interest with your school or other institutional organization.[24] If that was to occur, the school would need to provide you or your representation with a demand explaining the relevant contractual provisions that are in conflict.[25]

Contrary to FL, New Mexico's (NM) and Alabama's (AL) statutes allows its athletes to wear and endorse any brands that the student athlete wishes to wear and endorse regardless of the school's existing relationship.

Aside from the striking differences around a potential conflict, there are legal issues that must be explored which I will discuss later in Chapter 6, *The Legal Fiasco*.

<u>*Benefits of the Act to the Student-Athlete:*</u>

As you know, the ability to profit from your name, image, and likeness, has been an issue in the past.

Now, the legislation is finally here for you to use to your advantage and Florida's Act – as explained above – has laid out certain prohibitions to ensure that the student-athlete can profit from their name, image, and likeness unimpeded.

The Act also seems to promote and urge the student-athlete into understanding that he or she needs to hire professional representation for support, guidance, and navigation through this new entrepreneurial endeavor.

Furthermore, the Act provides that if you are attending a college on scholarship, that it is not deemed compensation for purposes of the Act, and it may not be revoked from the student for obtaining professional representation or earning compensation.

Although it's a long time coming for such law, honestly speaking, there are so many issues with the Act as written. It's silent regarding some major issues, such as athletes who are profiting from their names as a red-shirt freshman, or whether the student-athlete can serve a demand on their educational institution if it has engaged in a conflict of interest after the student-athlete's contractual relationship.

In any case, it is even more important that you establish the right team to help you navigate these newfound contours of entrepreneurship and foreseen legal challenges.

"Victorious warriors win first and then go to war, while defeated warriors go to war first and then seek to win."

~

Sun Tzu.

CHAPTER 5

Illinois N.I.L. Legislation & How It Differs

On June 29, 2021, Illinois took many by surprise, springing forward to become the very first state will full enacted NIL legislation for college athletes. I must say I was proud to be among leaders in the industry that spoke about that historic day with Chicago's ABC Channel 7[26].

Illinois is one of those rare states that represent all professional sports – soccer, football, basketball (women and men), hockey and baseball. Not to mention, Illinois also has some of the major universities that students dream of attending like DePaul University, Northwestern University, Loyola University, and University of Illinois (at Chicago) to name a few, so it goes without saying that I wasn't shocked to see proposed legislation in Illinois for student athletes to profit from their name, image and likeness ("NIL"). And, to top it off, Illinois's legislation took effect on June 29, 2021 – leaping ahead of many states to show its leadership.

Unlike Florida's NIL and other states like California and Colorado who have similar statutes, Illinois explains and defines what NIL means in legal terms, but also creates major restrictions for the athlete. Essentially, if student athletes aren't careful, they could run afoul of the statute and face legal challenges that could impact their bottom line.

So buckle up because this legislation has some twists and turns that you must make sure you're ready to tackle.

Illinois's Legal Definitions

What I love about Illinois legislation, which differs from regulations in FL, CO, and CA (to name a few), is that Illinois breaks down what Name, Image, Likeness, and a third-party licensee is. This is imperative to understand because what may seem to be a violation to a *lay person* ("an individual who does not know law") may not be. They could think that someone has violated their rights by misusing their *likeness*, when it could really be that their *image* was misused based on the statute's definition.

Suppose you filed a complaint against someone and pointed at the statute for support? If you didn't properly allege what the violation was, your matter would be dismissed for failure to state a claim. Hence, the importance of understanding legal definitions.

Illinois defines **Name** as "the first or last name or the nickname of a student-athlete when used in a context that reasonably identifies the student-athlete with particularity."[27] Think of it like this, names are written on a student's jersey. Your teammates may have a nickname for you that you've grown into or that the team has branded you with.

For example, Robert Griffin III – a former football quarterback for the Washington Football Team (formerly known as "Washington Redskins") was known as RG3. If I use myself as an example, my home nickname is "Vonnie" and a lot of people call me that but folks also know me as the "Protector of Athletes." Therefore, I can use my nickname to profit by licensing it out, or by showing up for appearances. Do you catch my drift?

Illinois defines *Image* as "any visual depiction, including, but not limited to, photograph, digital image, rendering, and video."[28]

Influencers come to mind when I think about this definition. Although athletes don't consider themselves influencers, think about the countless number of athletes in video commercials drinking an energy drink or carrying yogurt like New York Giant athlete Saquon Barley.

Companies may also want you to do a photo for digital or print ads which includes your image in a "digital" or "photograph" format.

Illinois further defines *Likeness* as "a physical, digital, rendering, or other depiction or representation of a student-athlete, including a student-athlete's uniform number or signature, that reasonably identifies the student-athlete with particularity."[29]

The former WNBA athlete, Renee Montgomery comes to mind. Recently, she posted on Twitter that she has released her NFT's and a beautiful commercial was created that included her Jersey ("Moments equal Momentum" (MEM)) but also had her signature with this array of light emitting from it. I'll also take this moment and honor one of my favorite cousins who died from bone marrow cancer years ago, Johnny Adams. We called him J-Red because he was light skinned with red hair and beautiful freckles that he got from his mom, Johnette.

Johnny played football and ran track for our high school. He landed a track scholarship with FAMU but was stricken with illness. Johnny was such an amazing athlete and wore the number 27 on his purple and white uniform that the school retired his jersey with that number. Now, when I visit my hometown of Gainesville, FL and see the 27 I think of Johnny ("J-Red") because it represents his likeness.

These definitions are important because as you make deals, you need to be clear on what aspect of your name, image, or likeness is being licensed or contracted on. This helps you to understand the scope of services and the compensation that should be rendered accordingly.

Now, Illinois defines a ***third-party licensee*** as "any individual or entity that licenses publicity rights or the use of name, image, likeness, or voice from any prospective or current student-athlete or group of student-athletes" and "shall not include any national association for the promotion or regulation of collegiate athletics, athletics conference, or postsecondary educational institution."

This is important to note because as a student-athlete in Illinois, if you want to make a deal to be compensated for use of your name, image or likeness, you can **only** do that with a bona fide third-party licensee which is defined by the statute.

LET'S TALK ABOUT THE MONEY!

Considering that student athletes are about to enter a new space that some people may be a bit upset because they haven't had to share the financial landscape with athletes. You need to discuss and define what the money is and isn't and who can and cannot pay!

One thing to clear up right off the bat is that Illinois – like many other states proposing and passing NIL legislation – is that compensation will **not** include scholarships, financial aid, room & board grants and the like. States differ however, on what will be considered compensation.

But we can all agree that NIL legislation is expressing that whatever student athletes realized from name, image, and likeness compensation, must be at the fair market value. Illinois adds that the student athlete's family cannot receive compensation based on the student athlete's name, image and likeness. This reminds me of the longstanding prohibition the NCAA has.

Illinois, as do other states like Florida, express that the student athlete may not receive compensation in relation to the athletes' athletic ability or for the potential of participating in a particular athletic association or school.[30]

ILLINOIS' PROHIBITIONS

Every state has its particular prohibitions or standards for student athletes expecting to take full advantage of earning income from their name, image, and likeness, but I found Illinoi's prohibitions or standards quite interesting.

A. Contract Terms

If you are a student athlete in Illinois or thinking of attending an Illinois school, you must note that there are particular time frames for engaging third-party contracts. In law, we call these timelines or deadlines "statute of limitations."

First, you can only have a contract if you are already a student at an Illinois postsecondary school.[31] Second, your third-party contract cannot begin prior to your enrollment.[32] Third, your third-party contract cannot continue beyond the participation in the sport at the postsecondary school.[33]

That latter provision makes me nervous because I ask the question(s): are we talking about the end of the season, the end of the student-athlete's athletic career and designation as a student-athlete, and/or after the student athlete graduates and is no longer considered a student athlete? Mmmm. I can see major problems with this and the determination of what would be legally considered *"beyond participation in the sport."*

B. Vice Brands

Illinois is not alone by prohibiting its student athletes from endorsing or receiving compensation for businesses or brands that are in the "gambling, sports betting, controlled substances, cannabis, a tobacco or alcohol company, brand, or products, alternative or electronic nicotine product or delivery system, performance-enhancing supplements, adult entertainment" industries.

You must keep in mind that some of the largest universities are State universities which mean they are funded by the Federal Government. Let's take cannabis as an example. Many states have legalized cannabis in a myriad of ways, but it's still illegal at the federal level. Therefore, the state is not going to pass a law for student athletes to profit from this sort of industry when that is in direct conflict with the federal government since that would threaten the school's funding.

I do believe, however, that banning certain industries helps the student athlete to focus on what's important instead of getting pulled into a deep hole that could threaten the student athlete's academics, athletic career, and life in general.

C. Conflicts

Illinois specifically forbids the student athlete to engage in any publicity rights agreement with a third party while the student athlete is engaged in school sponsored activities especially if "such services or performance by the student-athlete would conflict with a provision in a contract, rule, regulation, standard, or other requirement of the postsecondary educational institution."

I think about brands where the school already has a contractual relationship, but it could also mean that there's an internal rule or standard that the school has which prohibits such agreements. So, the student would not have the ability to enter in that particular agreement.

D. Disclosures & Mandated agreements

Illinois first states (as do other states) that the student athlete must disclose any agreements for publicity rights. However, Illinois expresses that the disclosure shall occur during the time frame created by the school.[34]

But what was even more thoughtful was that Illinois legislature adds that any compensation or value of service provided worth $500 or more must be in writing.[35]

This is important because of a legal concept called "Statute of Frauds." Statute of Frauds is a common defense to matters of contracts and what it means is that for particular issues like marriage, contracts worth $500 or more, services that cannot be performed within one year, and real estate transactions, such contracts must be in writing, or the agreement is unenforceable as a matter of law.

BOOOOOM! Technically, Illinois is helping the student athlete (in this particular area) protect him or herself from future unenforceable contract issues without even knowing it.

E. Representation

The student athlete is mandated to provided written notification and a copy of the representative agreement to the school within seven days of entering such business relationship.[36]

F. The School's IP

This area is interesting from an intellectual property (IP) – legal - aspect. Illinois prohibits the student athlete from entering into a publicity rights agreement that also includes existing registered marks, logos, verbiage, names and designs of the school.[37] Illinois does state, however, that the student athlete may gain permission for use, but the school would be entitled to compensation at market rate value.[38]

The IP world is extremely new for a lot of people and student athletes will have to learn about this quickly. Previously I stated that I understand why Illinois's legislature would include this because if the school has federally registered marks and all (or the majority) of students began to use and intermingle the school's marks with their brand and endorsements, it would weaken the strength of the marks that were federally granted to the school.

Therefore, there's a lesson to take from this. The student athlete should be just as eager to protect his or her marks as they are created and put into the stream of commerce. I'll talk more about Intellectual Property Rights in Chapter 10.

Embedded in this same section of the text is the following: "A postsecondary educational institution may also prohibit a student-athlete from wearing any item of clothing, shoes, or other gear or wearables with the name, logo, or insignia of *any entity* during an intercollegiate athletics competition or institution-sponsored event."[39]

Unlike a few states that welcome this sort of opportunity for student athletes, Illinois is saying "hold your horses!" Now, "any entity" is any person or brand that the student athlete may have an agreement with. But the limitation stated is during a competition or institution-sponsored event.

It's also important to note that this provision does not read as a mandate but as a permissive statement to the schools by inserting the word *"may also prohibit."* Therefore, the best course of action would be to determine what your individual school's rules are around this sort of thing and whether you're allowed to wear sponsored gear during school sponsored activities and competitions.

I know that this is such an exciting time for student athletes - but with that excitement is a lot of uncertainty. Moreover, if you are a student athlete who wishes to transfer out of a state like Illinois to Florida or from Illinois to a school in Alabama, it's going to be your responsibility to understand the rules and how you can use them to protect your interests.

In the next chapter I break down some legal issues that may or could result from current NIL legislation as we've come to know it and are getting acquainted with it.

"If we fail to adapt, we fail to move forward."

~

John Wooden

CHAPTER 6

The Legal Fiasco

As with any U.S. or State Congressional enacted rules, the state legislatures who are creating laws are sometimes not directly benefited by what they are drafting and passing or cannot fathom the impact that it will have in court. Because of that, legal issues will often pop up around what the legislature meant by a particular provision and the courts will have to make rulings to further expound on the meaning the legislature intended to give.

As more and more states pass NIL legislation and make it effective, each state will have rules that may be taken to court ("litigated") by students, state officials, sports associations, parents and others for guidance as to their rights and standing as it refers to NIL.

Taking that into account, there are some legal issues that may surface from NIL legislation based on what I've seen written previously between the student athlete, the school and/or school officials like coaches and other administrative staff.

Considering Florida's initial bold move to initially try to make their rules effective before any other state – and since I've talked about Florida before, let's stay with that.

Florida's Act mandates that a student athlete cannot enter a contractual relationship that is in direct conflict with their team contract or educational institution.[40] Note, that both Colorado and California's bills has very similar language.

Thus, the educational institution must disclose the provisions it believes are in direct conflict with the student's team contract to the student athlete or his/her representation.

This type of provision is a *conflict of interest* provision and the obligations on the school to provide notice is considered – a *disclosure* or *demand* of sorts.

Generally, and legally speaking, the student and the school are both dealing with certain intellectual property (IP) issues – i.e. brands. And, by way of those brands, either have had the benefit of entering or maintaining certain contractual relationships. When a party ends ups breaching or causes a conflict of interest, the other normally serves a demand asking them to stop. In the business world, this is called a *cease and desist* or *demand* letter.

These letters are important because they provide notice to the other party that they have done something wrong or engaged in some form of conduct that would cause immense harm to the other if they do not stop or course correct their conduct.

However, per Florida's Act (as are many other States NIL provisions), it's one sided in that it allows the school to serve a disclosure to the student if the student has engaged in conduct that amounts to a conflict of interest that could cause the school damages.

In contrast, the Act is silent as to whether the school can be engaged in a contract that creates a conflict of interest for the student athlete.

What would happen if the student athlete secured an amazing endorsement deal with Apple, Sony radio, or Dream Works publication for instance and subsequently, the school or its administrators secures a deal with the exact same brand and demands that the student ceases its contractual relationship because it's in direct conflict?

Here are the legal issues I see that the student athlete may successful allege: 1) retaliation, 2) violation of the statute by preventing the student athlete to profit from their NIL, 3) breach of contract, and 4) intentional interference with third-party contractual relationships.

VIOLATION OF STATUTE

Taking our little scenario into account, alleging a violation of the Florida Student Athlete Achievement Act ("FSAAA") (or CA and CO's similar provision, for example) may be plausible.

Particularly, under rule 1004.098, Section (1)(a)[41] the Act reads as follows:

> A postsecondary educational institution may not uphold any rule, requirement, standard, or *other limitation that prevents* a student of that institution from participating in intercollegiate athletics from earning compensation as a result

of the use of the student's name, image, or likeness. (emphasis added).

Additionally, under Section (5)(b)[42] of the Act, it reads as follows:

A student athlete who enters into a contract providing compensation to the student for use of the student's name, image, or likeness shall disclose the contract to an official of the postsecondary educational institution in which he or she is enrolled, to be designated by the institution.

California's similar section is listed in Section 2, Section 67456 (e)(2); and Colorado's can be found at Part 3, Section 23-16-301(3)(c).

There's a reason why I mentioned these two provisions. For starters, if you informed the school through its officials that you have engaged into a contractual relationship to profit from your NIL and they later enter into a conflicting relationship with your deal, this may serve as a basis for violation of statute by the school.

Furthermore, based on section (1)(a), if the school has engaged in some "other limitation" that prevents you – the student – from participating in intercollegiate athletics where you can profit from your name, image or likeness, this may serve as a basis for violation.

How? Well, for starters, when you disclose your contractual relationship and an official does something to prevent you from materializing that contractual relationship, it may serve as a basis for violation by the school.

Also, based on whatever the terms of your team contract were, it may contain language whereby if the student (you) is deemed to have engaged in a conflict of interest, you might be prevented from competing until you resolve the conflict. That would be a limitation – especially in bad-faith – if the school is limiting you from participating and profiting from a deal that you had first.

Although the Act is silent on these issues, it will more likely come to litigation to sort out what the intent of the legislatures was at the time of creating such rules and how they were intended to be resolved.

One thing to note, if you're in a state like Illinois, its NIL statute specifically expresses that it does not allow for a cause of action against the school or the athletic association.[43]

Let's discuss some legal issues that I see resulting from this legislation.

BREACH OF CONTRACT

You'll probably have signed a team contract that most likely forbids the school from interfering or preventing the student (you) from profiting off your NIL. Depending on what that contract provides, you may have a claim for breach of contract.

In a breach of contract case, you must first establish that you have a valid contract; and second, that the other party did something that breached (or broke) the agreement.

"To establish a valid contract, you have to show that the school made an offer (presenting a scholarship or team agreement for the student to come to its school versus another), the offer was accepted (by the student where she or he signs a scholarship or team agreement), and there was consideration (usually the amount provided in the scholarship or academic studies at $0 cost or discounted to attend the school)."[44]

Once you establish the validity of the contract, it's time to delineate how the other person violated (or breached) the agreement.[45] You do this by pointing to the provision in your agreement that was not met, and the conduct of the school (by its official) that supports the breach.[46]

If you have a written agreement that you can point to, to support your claim you'll want to pull that provision to the forefront and speak to why the school has violated it. Also, you can point to other issues under Title IX, Intentional Interference, and a violation of the statute as evidence to further support a breach by the school.

Now, what if you didn't have a written agreement with the school except for an Athletic Aid agreement[47] ("financial aid) that does not speak to any terms of the student profiting from his/her NIL; or considering prohibitions that would support a breach of contract by the school?

Can you make the argument that Florida's Act or some other state's Act creates a breach of implied contract? Implied means a conduct that is legal binding based on prior obligations. The answer is possibly, but the strongest argument would be to point directly to the statute's provision that was violated. Not all states recognize a cause of action for implied breach of contract.

You'd want to determine what course of action is provided by the statute in addition to remedies for the harm being caused.

It's also worthy to note that Illinois does not allow for any imposed liability to the school or the athletic association "related to its adoption, implementation, or enforcement of any contract . . ."[48]   You must take note of your state's particular prohibitions and any express language that details what liability will or will not be imposed because, if your state does not recognize or impose liability based on contract like Illinois, you'd need to find a separate area of law (and a separate factual basis other than the athletic contract) to bring an action if you believe you've been legally injured.

It's always best to consult with counsel even if you have a sports agent. Most agents are not lawyers and even if they are, you need a lawyer that can understand statute and has a background in contract law and litigation to ensure you're clear about your rights and obligations.

INTENTIONAL INTERFERENCE

There are various types of legal actions called *torts*. When someone commits a tort, this means that the person did something intentionally that caused direct harm to another. Based on our scenario, you could have an action for intentional interference with contractual relationships.

Specifically, in Florida for example, to assert a valid claim for tortious interference with contractual relationships, the student athlete would need to allege "(1) the existence of a business relationship under which plaintiff has legal rights, not necessarily evidenced by an enforceable contract; (2) proof of defendant's knowledge; (3) intentional and unjustified interference with relationship by defendant; and (4) damage to plaintiff as a result of interference."[49]

If we think back to our scenario you would be able to state a claim by alleging the following:

- that you engaged in a business relationship with brand-X to which you have a legal right to do per Florida's Act;

- that the school knew about the relationship which is evidence by the disclosure made by the student,

- that the school intentionally and without any merit interfered with that existing relationship by going behind the student's back and obtaining a similar relationship with brand-X, creating a conflict;

- and thus, the student has been damaged because the student is being denied the right to profit form their own NIL and

- and that the student is (possibly) subjected to other punishments if the student does not break up the contractual relationship he or she had prior to the school's relationship with brand-X.

But again, if you're in a state like Illinois, it specifically excludes any liability imposed on the school or athletic association for "tortious interference" claims.[50]

However, if you're in a state like FL which does not specifically exclude liability or this cause of action, an intentional interference argument would most likely be your strongest bet, but you'd still need to consider whether your school is immune from suit especially if you're attending a federally funded institution.

Now, I want to address an area of law that many people find confusion, *Retaliation* under Title IX.

TITLE IX: DISCRIMINATION

Given our scenario above where the school creates the conflict of interest and demands the student voids their agreement, this could be conduct in retaliation of the student. Let's take our scenario a step further: what if an African American female student athlete secured an amazing deal with ESPN to become a college sports analyst or became sponsored by Under Armour and the only reason the student received the deal is because these two platforms were seeking an African American female? Hmmm…

Let's take a look at this. Since the student athlete is not an employee of the school, we would need to lodge the argument under Title IX of the Education Amendments Act of 1972.[51]

The relevant provisions of the Act based on our revised scenario are the following:

> (a)… no person shall, on the basis of sex, be excluded from participation in, be denied the benefits of, or be subjected to discrimination under any academic, extracurricular, research, occupational training, or other education program or activity operated by a recipient which receives Federal financial assistance.[52]

> * * *

> (b) Except as provided in this subpart, in providing any aid, benefit, or service to a

student, a recipient shall not, on the basis of sex[53]:

(1) Treat one person differently from another in determining whether such person satisfies any requirement or condition for the provision of such aid, benefit, or service;

(2) Provide different aid, benefits, or services or provide aid, benefits, or services in a different manner;

(3) Deny any person any such aid, benefit, or service;

(4) Subject any person to separate or different rules of behavior, sanctions, or other treatment;

* * *

(8) Otherwise limit any person in the enjoyment of any right, privilege, advantage, or opportunity.

Under this rule of law, if you were an African American female athlete who secured an amazing brand deal or position with a third-party for purposes of profiting from your NIL and but-for being an African American female athlete you wouldn't have secured the deal, you may have a *prima facie* (clear-cut) case against the school for intentionally creating a conflict of interest that would deny you the rights to equal benefits or services.

Here's why. First, Title IX prohibits *recipients* who receive federal aid from engaging in conduct that would discriminate against others on the basis of sex in various forms.

Therefore, if you attend a state college or university, its likely they will fall under the requirements of Title IX.

Second, although Title IX applies to both female and male athletes, it's clear that if a female athlete is treated differently after securing a deal per a legal and unfettered right given to that student under the State's NIL statute and now the school is preventing or prohibiting that student from competing where she can further profit from her NIL, that will support a Title IX claim.

An argument can be made that the school is liable under (b)(3), (4), and (8) above by denying the student a benefit that she was entitled to; subjecting her to sanctions if she refuses to void her existing contract that allows her to profit from her NIL; and/or the school may be liable to the student from limiting the student from any right, privilege, enjoyment, or opportunity to profit from her NIL.

Here's another matter to consider: If the student is complaining that per Title IX she was treated differently or denied a benefit or opportunity that other male athletes on her team were not denied, she'll have to explain how the treatment is different by showing that it was based on her gender and that no other females were provided the same opportunities.

Another argument that the student may pose is that she felt she's been retaliated against by the school because she signed a deal with Brand-X.

The most important thing to remember when thinking you have a claim for retaliation is that it moves far beyond you "feeling like" someone has retaliated against you. Some behaviors may not be considered legal retaliation if you did not engage in a *protected activity* leading up to the retaliation. But beyond that, you must also show that you suffered an *adverse action* that caused your *damages*.

Let's break this down.

RETALIATION:

There is no specific retaliation provision under Title IX. Therefore, federal courts pull from Title VII (Civil Rights Act), for application of retaliation.

A little side note: Student athletes may think that they can allege a claim per Title VII based on sex and potentially race. The caveat is that per Title VII, you must be an employee to come within the statute. If you remember our discussions prior in this book, as a student athlete, you're not an employee of the school or athletic association. Therefore, that option is out, and all NIL legislation that I've read specifically excludes the student athlete from being categorized as an employee.

However, it is important that whomever you hire to represent you if something like this was to occur, understands Title VII and Title IX and parameters to support and protect your rights.

A. Protected Activity:

I often encounter all types of potential plaintiffs who enter my office saying: "I was retaliated against." One thing that they fail to realize is that there is no retaliation if you were not engaged in a *protected activity* by law.

Take our female student athlete for instance and the scenario we discussed above. A protected activity could be reporting and protesting the conduct that is prohibited by the NIL Act. But to truly establish that the athlete engaged in the protected activity would be to document the protest or complaint in writing, participate in investigations and such.

Although some people would wish to remain anonymous, that truly does not help your case if you are ever in this position, because you would be responsible for clearly establishing that you engaged in a protected activity and only after engaging in that activity, did you suffer a harsh consequence which we call an *adverse action*.

B. Adverse Action:

Now, imagine that you have reported numerous violations of sexual harassment, or mistreatment of benefits that other athletes of a different sex did not endure and because of your reporting, you were now removed from the team, banned from competing in an important game, or facing loss your scholarship. Simply, the action must be so material and adverse that you suffered because of it.

Let's say you lost your scholarship because of your previous protests and reports of the unwanted or biased treatment. Now, you're unable to compete athletically and unable to attend classes because you're unable to pay out of pocket costs for tuition. That's *material*. You may have the ability to sustain a Title IX claim in federal court for damages.

We can go a step further. Georgia (GA) has a provision in it's NIL legislation stating in part that:

> Team contracts may provide for a pooling arrangement whereby student athletes who receive compensation for the use of their name, image, or likeness . . . agree to contribute a portion of the compensation they receive pursuant to such contract to a fund for the

benefit of individuals previously enrolled as student athletes in the same postsecondary educational institution. [54]

Student athletes shall not be required to contribute an amount equal to more than 75 percent of the compensation received for the use of their name, image, or likeness.[55]

Now, just humor me for a bit - what if a particular school in GA decided to enact this provision requiring student athletes to put the cap (75%) of their earned NIL compensation in this general pool and the only student athletes to do that were from the Men's football and basketball teams?

Historically, we know that those major sports are comprised largely of African American and Hispanic players and typically the star players are also from these historically marginalized communities.

An argument could possibly be made that there is an adverse action because the school chose and implemented a blatant discriminatory rule requiring only these sports to contribute their earned NIL compensation to the student athlete pool which is enriching other student athletes who historically don't need the income.

Of course, it would be essential to show actual data from the school regarding the percentage of athletes on the team that are African American and Hispanic, how the pooling has impacted them created an adverse impact that illustrates direct discrimination in some way when comparing these particular students to other sports and their female athlete peers.

C. Causation:

Now, it's time to link both protected activity and adverse action together by establishing causation. Causation is the method of illustrating to the court that you engaged in a protected activity and only because of this, did the school adversely impact you. If you can do this, you may have a clear claim for Title IX.

D. Damages:

We discussed what damages would look like throughout the scenario, but I want to leave you with something in this section: *Just because someone does something to you that you don't like doesn't mean that you suffered damages.*

People outside of the legal community almost always forget about damages. Most people say, "I'm going to march in there and show them who I am" without any real way of measuring the harm that was done. If you're unable to establish your damages, you'll lose the case.

This is the big girl/big boy leagues now. Becoming an entrepreneur has many challenges and understanding the legal underpinnings of it all is paramount to your future success. Considering that litigation is always tricky and uncertain, it's important that you find the right attorney to help you through the planning phases and potential litigation areas of your building and protecting your NIL.

Always consider other options you have before resorting to court. If court is the route that you must take to promote and protect your NIL, make sure you keep detailed notes to fully support you. Regardless of what you choose to do, the most important thing is understanding your legal rights as a student athlete entrepreneur and conducting yourself as such.

For now, here are a few tips to Have Your S.A.E.™ as you're seeking endorsements, sponsorships, and other contractual deals:

Create a tracking chart identifying the company, the gatekeeper or agent, date the relationship was made, and the deal you are negotiating.

Ask your team official to provide you with a list of the school and/or teams endorsers, sponsors and affiliates so you can ensure you don't run afoul any standing student agreements.

When you have a signed contract for profit on your name, image, and likeness, notate the finalizing date on your chart in step one above, and notate the date you disclose such information to the school official.

When you disclose to the school official, make sure you describe in what format you provided the disclosure, and their response (if any).

And make sure you create a separate tracker for any issues you experience as a member of the team or school. These issues can be feelings or experiences of discrimination, harassment, and sexual harassment. You'll want to notate the people who witnessed certain matters happening, the date it happened, when you reported the issues, to whom you reported, and the final determinations made by the school official.

"It's okay to not know something. It's not okay to know you don't know something and yet, fail to fill the gap with expert professionals to help you guard your future."

~

Sivonnia L. DeBarros

Don't Put All Your Eggs in One Basket

Most student athletes (and hopefuls) think their dreams only begin with receiving a Division One (D1) scholarship at a NCAA school. Why is that? Most are told that they will be more visible if they played for a D1 school but fail to realize all the other important variables that go into "visibility" and earning a D1 scholarship.

Receiving a D1 scholarship is not the "end-all be all" of your sporting career or the only vehicle toward creating a successful name, image, or likeness (NIL) foundation.

First, have you ever thought about the amount of debt you'd incur when going to a D1 school especially if you're not on a full scholarship?

Second, you must also be eligible to play at a D1 school, meaning that you have taken the required courses and earned your grades, achieving a particular GPA to be considered for that Division. If you can't do that, why go to a D1 school that you may not be particularly ready or built for?

It's okay to start in another division or another athletic conference altogether. Growing up I only ever thought that NCAA was it. As I've grown older and considered other things, I saw other available options, I realized that student athletes have basically put themselves in a box.

Athletic conferences like the National Junior College Athletic Association (NCJAA or JUCO); and the National Association of Intercollegiate Athletics (NAIA) are a few associations that come to mind.

JUCO allows student athletes to receive degrees while also playing sports at a lower cost with more hands-on training, and with the benefit of smaller classes. NAIA provides student athletes with scholarships and smaller class sizes.

Both of those conferences remove the large price tag so the student athlete can focus on what truly matters – education. Without education, you will fail. It doesn't matter what it is! Mark my words, **you will fail**. I'm not saying education in the traditional sense as we know it in terms of sitting in a classroom. Why is that? Everything in this world centers around education. The decisions you make centers around education.

Regardless of whether you've worked hard to attend a NCAA, JUCO, NAIA or some other school, you still should understand why it's imperative to understand your eligibility, financial obligations, and rights under any NIL legislation that will directly impact you to fully build a solid foundation around NIL while at the collegiate level.

Get it out of your head **now** that you have failed if you cannot play at a NCAA school. That's not true. There are so many great athletes who have come out of NCAA schools and have nothing to show for it.

The same is also true for the opposite. There are amazing athletes who came from other conferences like JUCO and have found their place in sports and in the world like Albert Polhos (baseball), Sheryl Swoopes (basketball), Cam Newton (football), Bubba Watson (golf), and Jimmy Butler (basketball) to name a few.

It doesn't matter what conference or school you choose. You only have to choose what's best for you to make the most out of the NIL opportunities that are coming down the pipeline. How do you want to develop that? What impact do you want to make with it? What purpose will drive you forward regardless of where you are?

When you understand those things and you move forward FOR YOU, you will choose a school that will position and align with your overall purpose so you can Have Your S.A.E.™

But more than that, what's your attitude, because it doesn't matter where you are, *if your attitude is F**k'd up, ain't nobody going to want to deal with you!* Real talk! I tell people every day that "peace of mind" is everything for me. It doesn't matter how much money a potential client has when they come into my office. If they are going to be a big problem, I cut that cord early for sake of peace for myself.

I've seen documentaries where young people and athletes walk around with a grudge on their shoulder blaming all the people who are trying to help them instead of being thankful for the position that they're in. And I get it. I've been there – TRUST ME!

I went through so much in my teenage and early adult years that I carried that anger so deep inside. I remember an older adult telling me something that has stuck with me until this day. I can't remember their face or name but I remembered what they said. This person looked me in my eyes and said:

> *Sivonnia. It doesn't matter how good you are at something. If you always walk around with a nasty attitude, that's all people will remember and they'll never want to help you.*

I was like ... DAAAANG! It's been that bad? Rhetorically asking myself the question. I didn't realize that all the anger I harbored inside was reflecting outwardly so badly that it turned other people off and potentially, turned folks off from helping me.

I want you to remember that NO, I don't' want you to put yourself in a box and I don't want you to further isolate yourself from what could be an AMAZING future, because you've allowed a bad attitude and anger to overshadow all that was great about you.

Make sure you heal! Make sure you think bigger and further beyond the mental confines of anger and pain. Think larger than what team or one particular athletic association you want to play for. The picture is so much bigger than that. It's time for you to envision what you want your life to look like ten years from now.

YOU HAVE OPTIONS. So make this the best time of your life and choose wisely. Choose for you and not what you believe everybody else wants.

"Everything that is worthwhile in life is scary. Choosing a school, choosing a career, getting married, having kids – all those things are scary. If it is not fearful, it is not worthwhile."
~
Paul Tournier

PART-II

HELLO
PROPRENEUR

CHAPTER 8

When You Know Better, Do Better!

Let me holla at ya' real quick Young Blood. Okay, I know that sounds lame coming from a lawyer who grew up in the South. But for real, *let me holla at ya'* for a moment.

Have you ever heard someone in your family say, "when you know better do better" or that "common sense isn't that common to everyone"? I have. It's a staple phrase in my family.

The significance of the phrases is that those words played over and over in my head as I grew, up and even now as an adult married woman and mother. It's funny how you can hear certain things that stick to you like white on rice, and others roll off like a rain drop on a leaf.

What's my point? How many stories of pro-athletes did you hear before saying to yourself, "oh, I'm not going to do that"? Or "Yeah, she (or he) was dumb, that's definitely not me" only to go out into the world and make the same or similar mistakes?

It's okay to admit it. You must be real with yourself about this. We can look back over athletic history and see countless athletes who've made grave miscalculations with their decisions. They didn't understand this new concept of name, image, and likeness but it's been around for centuries.

When a professional athlete can retire and people still recognize them, they've created a *name* for themselves. When a restaurant creates a burger named after you or paints a portrait inspired by you, that's an example of your *likeness*. When someone uses you on a banner to promote their business, that's an example of your *image*.

We've been seeing this for a very long time, but I must admit, even I was tunneled vision with the "new bow" that's wrapped on the name, image, and likeness movement for student athletes, until someone recently asked me: "Does Name, Image, and Likeness only apply to college sports?" You should've seen me.

I almost leaped up from the couch to answer that until I realized I was on the telephone! But my answer was a resounding NO! Think about the ideas that have played around in your head when you saw or heard your favorite athlete was going to play on a particular day, or that your favorite team would be signing team memorabilia.

Those players built up an image, their own names, and built a reputation into the minds of the public that kept others liking them and coming back for more excitement. That's you! You have this beautiful name, image, and likeness already built in that you've been grooming for years, but there's only one problem, you haven't been protecting it.

Unlike the college athlete, you don't have to wait around for legislation to pass or for your athletic association to re-route and plan their rules to navigate how they will promote and protect your rights.

Everyone talks about making money! How much money you'll probably see. How much money you'll probably make over the next five years. How much money you'll make when you make a certain investment. But let me tell you this... the money won't matter if you're too busy to shift your mind, set accountability standards and educate yourself (as I said in Chapter 1) in order to protect what's yours.

Money is NOT the end all be all! Now you're probably saying to me, "only broke people say that." Nah. Besides people who are broke, real millionaires and billionaires also agree. There's one thing to remember about becoming an instant millionaire or a high six-figure earner – it didn't take years slowly climbing that ladder and seeing your pay growth increase each year.

As an athlete, you may have made $300k or $20M in just one paycheck. And I get it - how can someone say that you haven't become successful when you're holding checks like that in your hand?

Let me ask you this, how many athletes do you know who failed to set boundaries with their family, friends, and even those whom they trusted professionally? No matter how much money you make, it can disappear just as fast as you've earned it. That's why success must be deeper than making money or paying off someone else's bills! And with more money, comes more *potential* problems. If you have not rooted yourself in strong principles, it won't be the money that takes you down, it'll be YOU who does.

The other day while watching the NFL drafts, I heard a young brother say "today my mom is retiring." All I could do was put my hand on my forehead and think "here we go again." What if that lady doesn't **want** to retire? Why are you putting people in "financial crutches" by assuming all their responsibilities?

It's a great thing that a lot of these athletes want to try and reverse the financial strongholds that their families have been in, but it's not their responsibility to try to undo decades of mess that's been deeply rooted in the minds of those who've lived that way. One way you must protect your name, image, and likeness is through self-preservation. I've said this so much that I think people are probably tired of hearing about it. But it's true.

If you are willing to carry the deadweight of those who you know have been riding the coattails of your name, image, and likeness by name dropping you everywhere they go, that's not trying to do better. They are only looking for what the name and image of your athletic celebrity will get them.

And . . . when you no longer have that athletic celebrity and all the million-dollar checks stop rolling in, will you be able to count on these people? **Hell no, you won't** and I dare you to say otherwise. If they are looking at you now for everything, they'll be looking for another free meal ticket later, even if you're unable to provide it.

Something has to shift in you to recognize self-preservation protection and to kick it in drive. If you truly want the sustainable future, you believe you deserve, you must educate yourself and be accountable to yourself. Sports can surely give it to you, but it's up to you to nurture it, protect it, and grow it.

It's okay to have a conversation with your family and let them know that "I can't do what you're asking me. I can't fix all those years that people didn't want to take financial responsibility for their own shortcomings." You can say, "Look, I'm willing to get us all financial counseling and advice so we can grow sustainable wealth together and hold each other accountable around spending."

It's an honorable thing for athletes to want to take care of their families but I'm so tired of seeing them go down hard with nothing left because they couldn't say no. Because they felt that since "I made it it's my responsibility." NO IT IS NOT! Listen to me, "No it is not."

I can go on and on about the hundreds of athletes who've gone broke by biting off more than they can chew, spending more than they have to satisfy family and friends, but I won't. I just want you to recognize that it didn't take you becoming a Pro for people to recognize your name, image, and likeness but people will come at you differently now because of it.

Make sure you hire a competent attorney who will tell you what you need to hear - as opposed to what you want to hear - to protect your legal interests. Find a financial advisor who's transparent about how they get paid but do your own research too. You may also need a therapist. If your family is completely dependent on you financially, you need to figure out how this dynamic originated. Chances are, you're also dealing with some form of trauma that may cause you to lose all the stake you've built up around your name, image, and likeness and it's better to sort this out earlier on so you're not making decisions that are purely emotional, versus logical.

And get some damn insurance!!!! If your entire lifestyle is dependent on your strength and ability as an athlete, get insurance on it. Do you think a diamond dealer will buy large carat rocks to put them in the store front window and not insure them? Hell no. Do you think neurosurgeons who use their hands to save lives don't have insurance if their hands or brains were ever damaged? Nope!

Insurance is one of the fastest ways to grow wealth, but many people miss this income-generating opportunity for lack of education. And, if you're taking care of your family, you have an interest in them. It's okay to get insurance on them, so if something ever was to happen, they are covered because they are your investment. If you have children, not only can you insure your children, but you can insure yourself so that when you die, your children will be taken care of.

But remember when You know better, You do better.

"Everyone can rise above their circumstances and achieve success if they are dedicated and passionate about what they do."

~ Nelson Mandela

PART-III
Athlete Essential Convos

CHAPTER 9

Determine & Take Control of Your Brand

Y ou can ask anyone what they believe a "brand" is and you will most likely receive a myriad of answers. One thing I have learned is that creating, honing, and establishing a brand is something that takes consistent time and effort.

You're probably thinking at this point, "okay... so what is it and how do I determine if I have a brand"? Let me explain.

There are two types of brands you can create: (1) a personal brand; and (2) a business brand. I'll talk about these two interchangeably and differentiate where necessary. First let's define what each of these two means before we dive into actual examples and their impacts.

Your brand – at the most basic level – is you! It's what people think of you, how people perceive you, how you've presented yourself to others, and what you do every day, for example. No matter what you create, if you are the one behind the product, the cause, or the service, people will automatically feel a certain way (or have a perception) when it's associated with your name.

On a **business** level, the school you attend(ed) has a brand and has worked years to establish how other students and its alumni perceive it, for example. Most times, people will choose a school based on the percentage of students who graduate, who are professionally ready to enter corporate America upon graduating, information based on their athletic records, and the ability to possibly go pro, to name a few. If you're a pro athlete, your professional player's association has a brand and you've probably dreamed of playing for this organization for years – even as a kid – because of how they educated you on their brand.

Michael Jordan, for example, created a strong personal brand by illustrating diligence, respect, and an unmatched work ethic on and off the court. In his twenties, Michael took control of an opportunity and endorsement deal when he was approached by Nike in 1984.[56] Although his parents probably had something to do with his accepting an endorsement deal with Nike, nonetheless, he was a brand that Nike knew they needed.[57]

Nike distinctively understood the value that Michael had. They understood – not just the type of player he was – but who Michael was as a man. When Nike offered a deal to Michael, they gave him something that other brands probably weren't prepared to make at that time, and that was a shoe deal – the Air Jordan.[58]

Although Nike had projected that the shoes would possibly make $3 million over four years, the sales far exceeded their expectation in $126 million in the first year.[59]

Michael has since expanded his brand by owning the Charlotte Hornets.[60] When Michael purchased the company, it's value was low and was in extreme debt.[61] Michael made strategic moves and sold off a minority interest and the team has consistently profited since Michael took over.[62]

Now, let's compare Michael with a professional football player, now deceased, Aaron Hernandez. You probably know about Aaron's full story and how he was accused of several murders.[63] When Aaron was accused of murders, the Patriots jerseys that many roaring fans previously purchased subsequently lost its value. It's clear that Aaron's conduct and the allegations against him were so serious that it completely destroyed his personal brand, and the business around football for him.

The Patriots did a phenomenal job to ensure that its corporate brand did not sink along with Aaron's by allowing fans to swap their jerseys for something new! The fans wanted someone new to believe in and trust and the Patriots stepped up to accommodate them.[64]

Let's look at Colin Kaepernick as an example of a great athlete that used his name, image, and likeness for social justice.[65] He used the platform he had to show the world what he truly believed in – change for the greater good. Everyone knows Kaepernick as the football player that kneeled during the National Anthem because he could no longer deal with systemic racism against black and brown people and unjustified police killings of innocent black men and women.

Kaepernick was ridiculed by folks, especially Donald Trump, and others who decided to "not see" racism because – in my opinion - it didn't impact them. Yet, I digress because honey, that's another subject for a different book.

Kaepernick made a huge grandstand for his social justice beliefs and commitment, and it has truly paid off for him because he stood his ground for something that he believed then - and now.[66]

Let's review some athletes and entertainers who have either completely destroyed their brand, never quite understood what their brand was, or almost killed opportunities because they didn't understand the power of the brand.

Domestic Violence is a Brand Killer

The National Football League (NFL) has had their fair share of athletes who have engaged in domestic violence disputes. Remember Ray Rice, the Baltimore Ravens player?

Ray Rice was in an argument with his fiancé and hit her while in an elevator, which was caught on the elevator surveillance camera. You can see her on the video charging back at him. When she approached him, Ray hit her so hard that she fell and hit the railing. Then he dragged her – unconscious at the moment - out of the elevator. He had literally knocked her out![67]

After that incident, Ray was suspended for two games. Shortly thereafter, the NFL changed its policy on domestic violence, making a first-time offense punishable by a six-game suspension and a lifetime ban for a second offense of domestic violence.[68] As for Ray, his football career ended in 2014 when the Ravens cut him from the roster.[69]

Josh Brown, another football pro who played for the New York Giants, admitted to his team that he put his hands on his wife and that he held her down.[70] However, he claimed that he never hit his wife – who obviously – told a different story.[71] Eventually, Josh was cut by the Giants and just another example of pros that got in their own way and tarnished their brand, costing them big.

It amazes me at the opportunities provided young athletes and how they will find trouble that strips them of the amazing life they could've built for themselves. That brings me to Chris Henry which is an unfortunate and tragic story.[72]

Chris eventually died one day after falling off a truck; people believed his death was the result of a domestic dispute with a fiancé over the cost of their wedding.[73] Prior to that, Chris always had a volatile streak which caused him to be arrested five times in 28 months and eventually led to him being cut from the Bengals in April of 2008.[74] The Bengals had actually decided that they would give him another chance before the 2008 start year.[75]

Another example is Rae Carruth, player for the Carolina Panthers, who, in my opinion was downright evil, and I believe that caused him to lose everything including his freedom.

Rae was involved in a murder-for-hire plot to have his pregnant girlfriend killed.[76] The story is that Rae tried to kill the unborn child so that he didn't have to pay child support.[77] Insane, right? I mean, damn! The child survived but the girlfriend didn't. The child was born premature and suffers from cerebral palsy because of Rae's actions.[78] After spending 19 years behind bars, Rae was released.

Racism Damages Brands

Jake Fromm, a former Georgia Bulldog quarterback who was drafted by the Buffalo Bills made a racist and racially insensitive comment on a text when he stated that "guns should be expensive so that only elite white people could have them." [79]

His career was in danger and there were talks regarding cutting him from the Buffalo Bills roster. In hopes of saving his career and engaging in brand control, Jake issued the following apology:

> *I am extremely sorry that I chose to use the words "elite white people" in a text message conversation. Although I never meant to imply that I am "an elite white person," as stated later in the conversation, there's no excuse for that word choice and sentiment. While it was poor, my heart was not. Now, more than ever, is the time for support and togetherness and I stand against racism 100%. I promise to commit myself to being a part of the solution in this country. I addressed my teammates and coaches in a team meeting today and I hope they see this incident is not representative of the person I am. Again, I'm truly sorry for my words and actions and humbly ask for forgiveness. -- Jake Fromm* [80]

Another individual who has made racially insensitive statements is Coach Sylvia Hatchell. [81] Allegations arose about Sylvia telling her players that there would be nooses to hang them from trees. [82] "Although several parents' account of her exact words differed slightly, they all said that they heard her say "noose" and "tree." There was another incident where Sylvia had made a statement saying 'she should've known that she can't win championships with a 'bunch of old mules.'" [83]

At some point, Sylvia and her entire team was put on paid leave for an investigation to be made into the allegations.[84] Around April of 2019, folks were trying to determine if Sylvia would keep her job and if she didn't whether the school would still have to pay her beyond her termination.

Being a racist is not "cool" and will no longer be tolerated. This country and the entire world are craving change, and many are calling for others to suffer immense consequences for promoting, engaging, and supporting blatant – and under-the-table - racism.

Guns & Stupidity Kills Brands

Have you ever wondered what you'd do if you got the opportunity to become an instant millionaire? How you'd divvy up your funds? Put part in the bank, pay off some debt, etc.? Somewhere in the mix, try to make reasonable and responsible investments to build capital?

I do! I do very often. But when people do something stupid that threatens their entire livelihood, I can't do anything but say, "they did what?" Then I start talking to myself as if I'm talking to the athlete saying, "why the heck would you even do that?"

So, I had a dumbfounded look on my face when I remember seeing something flash across ESPN news about a pro athlete shooting himself in the leg. "Dude! For real!" was all I could say while yelling at the TV screen as if this athlete could hear me.

I am talking about Plaxico Buress, a New York Giants football player. Plaxico carried a gun inside a New York nightclub.[85] Somehow, his gun accidentally went off causing him to shoot himself in the leg.[86] Subsequently, and consequentially, Plaxico lost his job with the New York Giants.[87] Plaxico, through the help and aide of his agent, filed a grievance claiming that he did not get bonuses that he was entitled to receive, and which he won $1 million for that playing season and another undisclosed amount for 2008 roster.[88]

I always, ALWAYS, tell people to "do the right thing when no-one is looking." I say this because it's true. "What you do in the dark will come out in the light." Plaxico tried to hide that gun, but it still brought him down because there was nothing right about it in the first place.

Not Understanding Your Brand Will Kill Your Brand

Not understanding your purpose will lead you to destruction; you will continuously fall off course, causing you to course-correct each time. Starting over is never easy, but it's more defeating when every new start leads to disaster, simply because you didn't know your purpose or brand.

Think of Evander Holyfield for example. He is one of the greatest boxers of all times, but he's also extremely broke. His debt far exceeds his income because he never understood his brand outside of being a pro-athlete.

Holyfield had many "failed business ventures [that] included a record label which cost Holyfield $3.1 million, a restaurant business which cost over $10m and other products bearing his name including BBQ sauce, a kitchen grill and a fire extinguisher."[89] Had Holyfield set out a plan to determine what he was passionate about besides boxing, it might have helped him to map out prosperous goals that would take care of him in retirement.

Too often, folks do something just because other people are doing it; or engage in something because they want to make others happy. Or worse, make it look like they're winning when they're not, yet failing miserably.

You know what? "F" that for real! This opportunity is too precious to waste. This opportunity can be the meal ticket for the rest of your life to do something that shows the world that you're more than a jock!

And guess what? People love someone who's versatile. Remember, you're more than an athlete. Remember that and make a plan so you can maximize the future. Now that we've discussed ways to kill a brand, let's talk about what helps to build brands so you can take control of your name, image, and likeness like a Boss.

Integrity and Purpose Makes Brands

I'm going to say this again... What you do in the dark, will come to light. Therefore, be the best you! Do the right thing always. Carry yourself in a respectful manner so others are eager and hungry to invest in you.

I remember someone telling me a long time ago that people will help those they like. And... to add the cherry on top, if you are respectful, others see it. You don't have to literally yell it from the rooftop or walk around with this billboard asking for their help or support.

People who believe in good-hearted folks will instinctively want to help someone who is responsible, respectful, and diligent. Those character traits are a part of your brand because someone will want to invest in you – your personal brand – all because of how you carry yourself. And because of how you made them feel.

I know I've spoken about this before in this book, but it's worth repeating. There was a time in my life where I was angry at the world. I showed it in my interactions with others. I was slow to listen and quick to speak. I snapped easily at folks. It was the guidance that was poured into me that led me to understand that no-one will want to deal with a troubled girl.

To this day, I'm still fighting against the personal "rough brand" I created as a child and teenager, as some relatives will make certain statements although they don't know me now as an older and professional adult. I mean I'm 20 plus years or more removed from those rough edges and people will **still** want to remind me of mistakes I made in my teens. I didn't know any better then and did not have someone to give me the advice I'm sharing with you now. I didn't have a therapist or guidance counselor who would sit down with me to figure out what was behind that anger.

Something I've learned is that people will hold on to the most negative memories about you, completely ignorant of the amazing man or woman you've grown to be because they're comfortable having an idea of you that is inferior to them.

In my bestselling book, *What Are You Sporting About?©*, I emphasize knowing and understanding your purpose. When you create clarity around your passion and what your goal is in life, it will help to wash away the anger, the disappointment, the indecisiveness, and the bandwagon mentality because you will constantly be on a mission to accomplish the purpose within you. The purpose that you find will be your brand!

"A brand is the set of expectations, memories, stories and relationships that, taken together, account for a consumer's decision to choose one product or service over another."

~

Seth Godin

Intellectual Property Rights

Intellectual Property (IP) is an area that is most often confused and inadvertently transferred to other people giving them the opportunity to profit from your creativity, name, and image.

Before we dive in, it's necessary that you understand the three different types of IP: copyrights, trademarks, and patents.

Copyright protects written works like books, poems, presentations, art, and music lyrics to name a few. **Trademarks** protect the name of products or services in certain marketable industries. **Patents** protect a new process or methodology, like creating a novel app development process or a new medical device.

The most popular and common IP registrations are copyright and trademark protections. It always amazes me how often entrepreneurs and small business owners misunderstand the opportunity they have to profit from their IP rights and fail to properly protect their IP rights through federal registrations.

As a student athlete entrepreneur or *propreneur*, you must know and understand this opportunity as you go into unchartered territory. Therefore, your name, image, and likeness consist of intellectual property that you will need to safeguard and protect from unsuspected IP looters or by losing any protections afforded to you under law.

For instance, do you remember Kawhi Leonard, a popular Los Angeles Clippers basketball star? There was a ton of press surrounding a logo that he designed while in college and prior to signing an endorsement deal with Nike.[90]

Here's what happened. Kawhi left Nike and wanted to take his logo and property rights with him over to New Balance.[91] He sued Nike over ownership of the logo. Nike lodged their own claim against Kawhi alleging copyright infringement, fraud, and breach of contract.[92]

Although Nike never contests the fact that Kawhi did share an initial sketch with them when he was in college, they claim that they significantly improved the sketch and therefore, it's much different and superior to the sketch that Kawhi initially presented.[93] **See Fig. 1 below.**

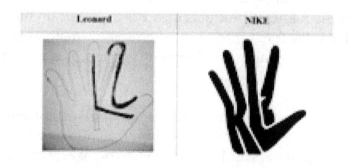

Figure 1: Sketches by Kawhi & Re-design by Nike
Source: Sports Illustrated[94]

To make matters worse for Kawhi, in 2014 he admitted in a story about the Klaw design that Nike significantly improved the designed and that he completely depended on their team to get things done.[95]

Athletes, and people in general, always underestimate the power of legal support. Look at Kawhi's issue for example. It's important to have legal representation at every stage of your entrepreneurship journey, because it will help ensure that you put certain contractual safeguards in place to help you avoid making statements in writing or on video that will come back to bite you later, and simply to create checks and balances for each phase of creating and developing your IP.

Kawhi has lost ownership in his IP, the Klaw logo, possibly for a number of reasons: (1) he failed to understand that simply creating a drawing does not give him an unfettered right or interest in that property; (2) he most likely didn't have an *assignment of interests* agreement with Nike (which I'll discuss soon); and (3) he most likely didn't protect his property interests through a buy-out or buy-sell agreement.

No Unfettered Right In IP

I know you're saying: "how in the heck does he not have an unfettered right when he's the one that created the logo in the first place?" and I totally feel you on this.

Let me explain. Many IP owners – whether it be a logo, a blog article, a process, a brand name, a course, etc. – do not have an unchallenged right in that creative property, especially if they have allowed others to work on and advance the property.

When IP owners engage others without proper agreements in place which fully delineate who owns what, and include "but-for engaging in this agreement for purposes of improving Brand-X," the law would generally see the IP owner and the person making improvements on Brand-X as both owners of IP.

Therefore, those actions – without proper safeguards – inadvertently tenders interest in the IP created, maintained and improved to belong to the person you allowed to engage on the brand. Of course, there may be additional arguments around this but essentially this – in my opinion – is what happened to Kawhi.

He created the Klaw logo and when he signed an endorsement deal with Nike, he – like most eager young professional athletes – possibly didn't read the fine print to make sure he protected himself regardless of whether they made improvements on the design.

And let me be clear – there's no damn way I would have ever admitted on a public stage or record that anyone helped to "significantly improve the design." I mean that was just crazy to me. But of course, I'm a lawyer so I see problems where others see it as simple innocence and naivety.

Kawhi's statements coupled with Nike's arguments of significant improvements of the design, promoted Nike's position and it's argument that it is the sole owner of the Klaw design – not Kawhi.

Hypothetically, even with the significant improvements, Kawhi could have entered an *assignment of interests agreement* or included a clause about retaining ownership of his IP interests with Nike.

IP Assignment of Interest Agreement/Clause

An IP Assignment of Interest Agreement or Clause simply asks the person or company you hire, retain, or partner with that "but-for" their expertise in doing "X" they would not have been retained to help build, create, improve "Brand-X." Thus, the person or company that the IP owner hire, retain or partner with agrees by entering this agreement that the original IP owner owns all of work created and improved by the other.

Now, here's the caveat. These agreements will not go over lightly without a showing of substantial consideration. *Substantial consideration* is something that you give a person in exchange for their work or support. $1.00 is not enough to show substantial consideration.

Let's use Kawhi's story as an example. Hypothetically speaking – since I do not know the full details surrounding his partnership or endorsement deal with Nike – Kawhi could have probably paid Nike substantial consideration by not electing to take any net sales from revenue received from products with the Klaw design until Nike receive "$X" amount of money first, which would be compensation for the work on the logo.

As another example, Kawhi could've paid Nike "$X" amount as a pay-in to their partnership or agree to engage in several interviews on Nike's behalf valued at "$X" as substantial compensation.

Either way, I'm not privy to the entire situation, but the moral of the story is to stop giving your ideas away for free. Stop asking people to do this or that for you if you're not willing to put proper safety measures in place to retain complete autonomy and control over your brand.

Buyout or Buy-Sell Agreement

Another way you can protect your IP interests by agreement, and how Kawhi could have possibly included another safety measure, would be to create a buyout or buy-sell agreement with your partner – or anyone you believe may have some inadvertent interest in your IP.

A *buyout* or *buy-sell agreement* is a document, or contract clause – where the parties determine what would be triggering events to either buyout or be bought out. This agreement should also state what interests the parties have and how such interests should be valued at the time of the breakup.

Now, we do know from the news that Kawhi's relationship with Nike was not a "happy go lucky" type of split. Therefore, I'm curious to know if the parties ever entered a buyout agreement, had they ever discussed the value of interests, and who would own what if either party exited the relationship.

By everything that happened, I'm guessing they didn't. If they did, Kawhi would have known what interests he retained in the Klaw logo and whether Nike would pay him a percentage for complete control upon his exit, or whether he would pay Nike to buy out their interest so he can use the logo he created without incident and issue.

I always tell my business and athlete clients to stop allowing folks to volunteer or work on your craft without having these agreements in place. Kawhi's Klaw logo is a huge and recognizable brand in sports, and it's a sad situation that he has lost it all at this point.

"We try to keep tabs on our intellectual property, but sometimes it's difficult to make sure that infringement isn't happening. When it does, it's your work that's at stake, and you have to do what you can to protect it."

~

Jill Stelfox

CHAPTER

11

Right of Publicity

According to the Intellectual Property Magazine[96], there are 31 states that recognize a Right of Publicity either through statute, common law, or a combination of the two.

What is *Right of Publicity*? Historically and commonly, it is a person's right to have first dibs on their own image and likeness for commercial gain. Therefore, when someone wants to use your name, image, or likeness for commercial gain, generally that person is required to secure the right to use your name, image, or likeness for that purpose.

For purposes of discussing name, image, and likeness in the era of college sports and pros, let's discuss how this can impact you. Colorado (CO) is one of the few states that does not recognize right of publicity by statute. What does that mean for a student-athlete in Colorado with a great following and brand around his or her name? What does that mean for a pro athlete?

It could mean a few things. What if you are playing for a school or professional sport organization that's located in a state that recognizes a right of publicity? You've received endorsement deals, sponsorships or built very lucrative business relationships because of your name and image.

Now let's say that someone in another state – where right of publicity is recognized – uses your likeness in some way for commercial gain without your permission. What harm does that do to you? Let's take this piece by piece.

First, who's the person using your name, image or likeness for commercial gain? This is important. Sometimes, people get so litigious – meaning, wanting to fight over something that may be better suited with a conversation – that they lose sight over the fact that you possibly could create a new business relationship and ask for a cut of the revenue.

If the person or business entity is already promoting products with your name, you should first have your legal representative reach out to determine the extent of commercial gain and how they are using your name, image and likeness (i.e. your brand).

Secondly, once you determine who is using your name, image and likeness and your representatives have reached out, they should then schedule a meeting. This could be a discovery meeting to learn more about the other person or business entity that's using your name and determine if this is a brand that you may want to do business with.

If so, this is a negative issue that has now turned into an opportunity. You can discuss the matter with you counsel to work up a proposal to enter an endorsement, sponsorship, or affiliate type relationship and ensure that you receive a percentage of the proceeds received for purposes of using your name ("brand").

If you and your team have determined that this person or business entity's image does not line up with your image and what you want to portray to the public, your team can demand – preferably through a demand letter- that they cease using your name, image, or likeness by specifying the time allotted for them to make changes and the consequences that would result if they refused.

Now as an example, if you lived and played in CO, there is no direct statute in Colorado allowing you to bring a claim for violation and damages based in Right of Publicity. However, it may be possible to seek damages in the state where the culprit resides and does business.

It's always necessary to have legal representation on deck to help you sort through the legal challenges and police your brand. For a long time, people have had the ability to use student (and pro) athlete's names, images, and likeness for purposes of commercial gain without any legal ramifications.

Think of this: what if the local burger joint used your name for a new burger creation and put your picture on the menu beside it. Technically, it may be a statutory violation, but it also may not be much to fight over. Not to mention, each state will apply their statutes differently and the amount of damages that you may be able to seek will also differ from state to state.

Florida and California have Right of Publicity Statutes. Let's take a look at them to understand how these statutes can provid additional protection for your brands.

CALIFORNIA & FLORIDA RIGHT OF PUBLICITY STATUTES

Upon a simple reading of both statutes, it appears that both Florida and California have statutes that prohibit others from using a person's name and likeness without consent.

Here's a brief statement of **California's**[97] statute:

(a) Any person who knowingly uses another's name, voice, signature, photograph, or likeness, in any manner, on or in products, merchandise, or goods, or for purposes of advertising or selling, or soliciting purchases of, products, merchandise, goods or services, without such person's prior consent, or, in the case of a minor, the prior consent of his parent or legal guardian, shall be liable for any damages sustained by the person or persons injured as a result thereof. ...

* * *

Florida's statute[98] reads in part as the following:

No person shall publish, print, display or otherwise publicly use for purposes of trade or for any commercial or advertising purpose the name, portrait, photograph, or other likeness of any natural person without the express written or oral consent to such use...

* * *

As you can see from the opening text of both statutes, there are some differences but many similarities. Although California statute mentions "minors" in the beginning, Florida's statute discusses that later in their statute.

One thing to note though is the differences between allowable damages per statute.

California's right of publicity damage provision specifies that the injured party or parties can seek damages equal to the greater of $750.00 or the actual damages suffered PLUS any profits that were derived from the unauthorized use. It's important to note that the "profits received" during the illegal acts is not computed as actual damages.

Additionally, California provides a right to attorney's fees and cost in bringing an action based on statute. Their statute also reminds the reader that the remedies are cumulative which will be taken into account with any other damages provided by law or statute.

Therefore, seeking damages in California based on statute will look something like this:

$$= \underline{\quad X \quad}$$

< of $750 or Actual Damages

+

Attorney Fees

+

Cost

+

Other damages by common law or statute

+

Profits derived from unauthorized use

In Contrast, Florida's statute provides the right to bring an action for injunction to stop a person from engaging in unauthorized use or to bring an action to recover for damages resulting in loss or injury. Those damages can be loss of reasonable royalties you would've received and punitive or exemplary damages.

Punitive generally means to punish the wrongdoer. *Exemplary* is similar but besides punishing, it's to make an example. Both types of damages are designed to deter future behavior from the wrongdoer or someone who is thinking of participating in the same type of conduct.

Florida's statute, like California, does inform the reader that all these damages are meant to be cumulative and in addition to other damages that may be afforded to the injured party. Although Florida's statute does not specify – as California does – in providing for recovery of the profits received during an unauthorized use, Florida does specify that you can recover damages for "*any loss.*"

Therefore, keeping "any loss" in mind, seeking damages in Florida based on its statute may look something like this:

Injunction + Action = X

Profits derived from unauthorized use
+
Reasonable royalty
+
Punitive/Exemplary Damages
+
Attorney's Fees & Cost
+
Damage to Goodwill/Name

You're probably saying to yourself: "how can she add the attorney's fees, costs, and the damage to goodwill and name when it doesn't say that by statute?"

I'll tell you why. It's called good lawyering. Go in swinging and hit something. If the statute says "any loss" then these things may be considered a loss recoverable by the statute. Of course, there may be case law that further defines what "any loss" means, but your counsel would have done the requisite research and work to counsel you accordingly.

For someone who is not a law student or doesn't have a desire to become a lawyer, you might also be asking yourself, "why do I need to know this?" You must be mindful that you are in business. You are – after all – an entrepreneur. People will try to take what they can get from you before you know what is going on. Some people will try you just to see if they can get away with it. And if you let them, it will send a message to your community and beyond that you're not ready - that you're not serious about your business and you lack credibility.

As I have mentioned numerous times throughout this book, it's time to conduct yourself as a businessperson. You cannot create a brand around your name, image, and likeness and leave it tossed up in the wind for anyone's gain. No. You must police it with business savviness, assertiveness, and grit necessary to create the success you desire.

"Avoid the crowd. Do your own thinking independently. Be the chess player, not the chess piece."

~

Ralph Charell

CHAPTER 12

Safeguard Your ASSets

Listen. Please forgive me if this chapter has me expressing my own feelings a little. This is one area that I'm extremely passionate about because it frustrates the hell out of me that people WILL NOT LISTEN to adequate advice but will be the first in line to operate sloppy businesses and brands without thinking about the consequences.

Here we go. I have consulted with, advised, and represented many small business owners and entrepreneurs who – to express it simply – didn't know what the hell they were doing. Their ideas and type of business were good, but the lack of planning, creating structured agreements, and seeking professional advice early on contributed to liability – and for some – demise.

Listen to me carefully! I do NOT want that to be you. As a smart athlete entrepreneur, it's important to have critical input about your brand and a say about what direction you may want to go in and how you want to build it for the future.

In the same breadth, it's also imperative to know when you are "in over your head" and need help.

No-one can do everything alone. We all need necessary support and guidance. We need certain skilled professionals around us to challenge us, keep us on track, to educate us, and help us maximize our present and our future.

But! And it is an important but! If you are too prideful to discern when you need additional help, undoubtedly, problems will arise, and your ship will start to sink. This is the time to plan for your entrepreneurship journey, but it's also the time to recognize how you will safeguard your **Assets** from looming liabilities and other detrimental consequences.

Have you ever wondered why so many pro-athletes and celebrities go broke? Well, if you didn't, I'm going to tell you anyway. **Taxes**! Let's talk a little about that.

'Dem Damn Taxes!

Good ole' Uncle – Damn - Sam be waiting for his coins! As an athlete entrepreneur, if you sign any endorsement or sponsorship deals and are paid for your name, image, and likeness, you will have to pay taxes on that.

As a pro athlete, even if you lived in a location where there are no state taxes, you'd be required to pay state taxes in States where your away games were played. This can get costly and tricky for professional athletes.

You cannot avoid Uncle Sam. When your endorser or sponsor pays you, they are reporting what they paid and to whom. You will have already provided a signed tax document to them for proof of their payment. It is deductible to them because it's a business expense.

Therefore, let's say you receive a value of $30,000.00 or $50,000.00 (just for example), that will yield a pretty high tax penalty.

Rhetorical question: Do you want to end your success before it can get started? Of course, you don't. Therefore, if you are earning moderate to high profits from your name, image and likeness, it's best that you form a legal business and hire a CPA and an accountant to help you navigate the tax and legal ramifications.

Often, pro-athletes and celebrities spend too much and never plan for taxes. Some pro-athletes have lost everything because of horrible tax and financial planning. I hate to tell you, but taxes are something you cannot escape. You need to retain the right help to show you how to maximize your income by using the tax code to off-set tax liability.

Now, if you create a legal business, you will enjoy certain tax benefits, like business deductions, that you wouldn't have as an individual taxpayer. Therefore, minus a business, if you profited $30,000.00 to $50,000.00 on your name alone, you'll be paying 100% in taxes on that income.

Register a business and any expense you incur for purposes of your name, image, and likeness as it relates to your business profits will be deducted from what you earned for purposes of taxes. You can also make donations in your business name that can be used as a business deduction in the year incurred. All of this will help your tax liability to shrink. I'm not a CPA so I urge you to retain one.

Create A Business

You can listen to street lawyers if you want to do that but don't come running back saying "you told me so." Street lawyers think they have the right legal advice, but never passed a Bar Exam to save their lives. Or practiced law.

Here's a crash course on the different types of entities that are applicable to you. (*See Athlete Entrepreneur Resources for Business Entity Chart* for a full list on different business entity types at the end of this book).

The most popular business formation that people know is the **LLC – limited liability company**. But what many people don't know is that an LLC is a pass-through company, meaning that income made to the business is passed through and taxed to the company's owner(s) for tax purposes, unless there is a tax election seeking to be taxed differently.

If you're a sole member-managed LLC ("i.e. only owner of the business"), what you made for your business will "pass through" and be taxed on your individual taxes but you still have the benefit of business deductions and other donations made.

You could file as an LLC and take a tax election to be taxed as an **S-Corp**. An S-Corp is one of the two types of Corporations, but this one elects to pass corporate income, losses, credits, and tax deductions to its shareholders. Notably, any distributions made to the shareholder(s) from the corporation can be made tax free if the distribution was already taxed. I know… this stuff is so technical which is why you need to establish a team to help you navigate what's the right call for you.

Note, the difference between an LLC and a Corporation is that an LLC is a company requiring at least one member or manager when filing a registration, and a Corporation is a corporation requiring at least one shareholder when registering. An LLC is formed, and a Corp or S-Corp is incorporated.

A **Corporation** or as many have termed it, a C-Corp requires at least one issued stock and one shareholder to incorporate. However, one of the differences between it and an S-Corp is that it receives more tax benefits, such as fringe and dividend deductions. Additionally, C-Corps are not pass-through entities. They are taxed once to the owners or shareholders, and once to the corporation.

Sole Proprietorship. You can listen to Your Uncle, Auntie, Cousin or friend if you want to! If you decide to march your butt down to the state's Secretary of State (SOS) and file a form for sole proprietorship, you might as well stay home.

A sole proprietorship does not give you any tax benefits or any legal protections from liability. A sole proprietorship just basically says that you're acting as if you have a business – but you don't. Sole proprietors are taxed 100% as an individual and cannot deduct any expenses they incurred for "their business."

You may have heard folks say to go file a **DBA** along with the sole proprietorship. A DBA means "doing business as" and is simply a nickname for a company or brand that it wants the public to call it. It's just like having the name your parents gave you at birth, but your friends and close relatives call you a nickname – but for business.

Just like a sole proprietorship, a DBA is not a legal business entity. It does not give you tax benefits nor does it shield you from any liability. Once I represented a club owner and he had lawsuits from everywhere. He had multiple club locations with different names. When I looked up the business registrations, I recognized that he never registered these entities as separate business entities. He only gave them business nicknames. Therefore, he was unable to limit his liability from one location to another. What do I mean by that? When you are sued in your business, if there is not a clear and legal separation between your "businesses," those legal battles may (and most likely) will impact the financial stability of the other business assets you have.

This is why understanding business formation is important. These are not all of the different types of business entities, but these are the ones that I believe you might have more questions about.

Now, that we have gotten some of the heavy stuff out of the way, what about those contracts? Contracts are a missed opportunity to safeguard your assets.

Contracts

As an athlete, not only do you Have Your S.A.E.™, but you need to conduct yourself as an actual business owner. If someone wants to do business with you and you have reached an agreement, follow it up in email and then submit a proposed written agreement. (*See Chapter 12, Get Your Contracts In Order*).

It used to be okay for people to do business on a handshake because folks truly did go by the saying "my word is my bond." Nowadays, people are looking for the loophole, and your sloppiness, to gain a "one up" on you. Trust me, you don't want to be looking at a failed opportunity simply because you didn't do enough to cover your Assets.

Many entrepreneurs and business owners have walked in my office asking for help and presenting either a sloppy agreement or none at all, and then expect miracles to be performed.

When you see what you think you agreed to in writing, it should cause you to pause and think: "Is that what we really talked about? No, this isn't what we agreed to." As opposed to you fighting years later about what both of your intentions were at the time.

Getting your agreement in writing should always be one of your first steps to ensure that you understand what you're agreeing to, and what your rights and obligations are under the contract.

Financial Advice Is Key

Now, if you are truly profiting from your name, image, and likeness, it's best practices to find a trustworthy financial advisor to help you manage your finances by setting up tax deductible retirement plans and finding other ways to create financial stability. I know… that's not fun. You want to do what every other big-time athlete does when they sign or enter a great deal. You want to take people out for dinner, buy an expensive car, pay off your mama's bills etc.

But listen to me. Don't do anything until you have spoken with a financial advisor who can tell you how you can maximize your income and still possibly do some of those things that you want to. However, if you do not plan, you will find yourself stuck. The same thing goes for finance.

This is an exciting time for any athlete! And for student athletes, how I wish the same opportunity existed when I was in college! But you're in the big leagues now. You have to think smarter.

Being an athlete creates more responsibility than your peers. You're in business! A brand builder! A future creator! You have to – and must – safeguard that.

"In life there will always be people with proposals to curb, to block your way. Please, go against the Current. Be courageous, COURAGEOUS: Go against the current."

~

Pope Francis

CHAPTER 13

Contracts On Lock

Do you know the number of people that enter medium to large deals on a regular basis and never, never, NEVER, consult with counsel?

Do you know the number of people that enter some type of deal and never even get it in writing? I mean, c'mon man! Having a contract in tow is one of the smartest things you can do. No... it's not bullet proof, but it's darn sure better than having nothing.

Since you are well on your way to becoming this unstoppable Athlete entrepreneur in *beast mode* around your name, image, and likeness (NIL), I want to share some of my major contract provisions that you should always make sure are addressed.

THE PARTIES

I have seen all sorts of contracts but what baffles me most are agreements that only state one of the parties' names and not the other; or get this - no-one at all.

Your agreement should clearly identify who the parties to the agreement are. Not knowing who's supposed to be bound by the agreement will likely result in a timely and costly case to prove to a judge or jury that you were entitled to a certain thing or service.

DURATION

Do you want to be in a contract that's locked in indefinitely? Maybe not. You should make sure that your agreement has a clearly defined start and end time. It's okay to say that the agreement will automatically renew upon some trigger timeline or another.

Without clearly defining this provision, you may set yourself up for failure if you engage in prohibited conduct outlined in the agreement and the contractual term is not over.

That takes me to my next point.

TERMINATION

You should always have a provision that speaks to when and how the contract can be terminated. If the contract does not automatically terminate upon the completion of something or the coming of a deadline, you want to know how you can exit the relationship without penalty.

Some provisions have called for a mutual agreement in writing to terminate the relationship early. I've seen some provisions say that either party can freely terminate the contract by written notice to the other within a certain time period.

Whatever your prerogative, just make sure that there's a way out of the relationship so you're not stuck in arms with someone who is making it hard to do business.

BUYOUT

Another provision, similar to a termination clause, is called a buyout. A *buyout* provision allows the party to determine how and when the other party can "buy out" or be bought out for whatever reason. This type of provision forces the parties to think about how their product/service/brand will be valued and what type of formula will be implemented earlier into the relationship rather than later.

Buyout provisions are especially valuable if you've created IP and have provided immense value to a company or brand. This sort of provision allows you to ensure that there's always a way to exit, knowing exactly what it may look like for you in terms of assets or income.

FORCE MAJEURE

Most people do not have *force majeure* provisions in their agreements. "Force majeure" is French and means superior force. This legal concept has been used to protect parties from performing if something beyond a party's control has made it difficult or impossible to perform.

For example, if you were already in a contractual relationship with a Brand Sponsor that required to make four media appearances wearing Brand Sponsor's logos or talk about its products during the Summer 2020, this provision would allow you to cancel the agreement. Or vice versa, since Covid-19, the Brand Sponsor canceled your appearances making it impossible for you to comply with your contractual obligations by triggering the force majeure provision.

But on the flip side, the Brand Sponsor could argue that force majeure is not applicable if the media companies will still give you the features through other digital platforms since everyone is working remotely. You may still have a contractual and legal obligation to perform under the terms of your contract.

Be mindful, however, that this provision is not to be taken lightly. Sometimes things beyond your control may present that forces you to violate the agreement. But, you would be pointing to this agreement and saying "Hey, I can't perform because it's literally impossible for me to do so at this time" and therefore, there's no technical breach.

COMPENSATION

Normally, people think of compensation as the giving or receiving of money. You can be compensated in all types of ways, such as through bartering (giving a product or service in exchange for a product or service), compensated by the value of certain product or endorsement, or free publicity, to name a few.

Regardless of what form of compensation will be provided to seal the deal of your agreement, you need to specify with particularity what the compensation is, when is it to be received, who will provide it, how much (if money or product), and the frequency of receiving such compensation.

You always want to make sure that when you do your part, the other person is also doing theirs. Therefore, never leave yourself hanging by creating this blanket statement that a person is supposed to give you X of product or money in exchange of you doing something that's supposed to earn X amount each time you perform.

This is a pure example of people entering agreements without counsel, thinking they understand what they are entitled to without knowing that they've extremely limited their worth in some way. You should be very clear on what your compensation is to look like. For example, "Joe Blow agrees to receive $10,000 in exchange of two media appearances through digital, video, or televised on or before x-date."

SCOPE OF SERVICES/ENTITLEMENTS

This provision is important because it speaks to what the parties are receiving in exchange for certain compensation. It also helps as a resource that you can reflect on to ensure that you have either received all that the other party promised to provide, or that you've provide all that you promised to give.

Be mindful that some people try to "scope creep" you in your deal. Scope creeping is someone who uses the initial contract as an avenue to get more service, product, etc. out of you although the agreement does not call for it.

Best practices are to always reflect on the scope of services provision if the other party is asking for something in addition to the initial agreement. That way you can refresh your memory, can either modify the agreement to include the request, or flatly deny it.

INTELLECTUAL PROPERTY

Now, although I'm including this provision here, it's possible that you may not need this provision if the person entering a contract with you is not helping you or using your intellectual property (IP) in any way.

Considering that name, image, and likeness is essentially IP, it is good practices to speak to what's considered authorized and unauthorized use of your IP, according to the terms of your contract and the objectives you're trying to achieve.

I cannot stress enough the need to police your IP. If you have a recognized trademark or copyright and don't ensure that people aren't infringing on them, your IP could become weak, losing the ability to receive full federal protections. I think it's also worth noting that if you have great developed and recognized IP, you may want to create a separate IP agreement so that everyone is clear on what they can use, how often and at what cost.

NON-COMPETE

You've probably heard the term "non-compete" mentioned before but weren't sure what it was. It's simply a clause that says you or the other party agree to not compete with each other in a certain place, during a certain time period (during, or after the agreement's termination), and in the same industry.

State laws dictate the exact guidelines that are necessary to ensure your non-compete clause is legally binding and will not be stricken. For instance, in Illinois, the rule is that the non-compete has to be geographically limited in scope, have a reasonable duration, and specifically state the type of prohibited activity.

For instance, if you entered an agreement with a teammate to build radios and then sell them, it would be unreasonable to limit the teammate's ability to enter a separate agreement later that's in an entirely different state, five years after the conclusion of your agreement with that teammate, and where you have indicated that the teammate cannot build radios, sell or do anything involving radios. Something like that would inevitably not be given any weight and stricken by law.

Non-competes should be taken very seriously regardless of who is seeking to have one signed. Non-competes are also a great way to protect your IP and protect yourself from unfair competition when doing business with someone who then seeks to use your IP for unilateral compensation. In a situation like that, and especially if your creation is novel, you may be reasonable in restricting the competition or use of such IP even if this happens in a different state. It all depends on your contract. That's why having legal representation is imperative to your protection and success.

JURISDICTION

A lot of people fail to discuss which state would have jurisdiction if these issues surfaces. Of course, this may not be a problem if both of the contracting parties live and work in the same state.

We live in a world where products and services can easily transcend state boundary lines. Therefore, you want to think long and hard – and preferably with the advice of counsel

- regarding which State should have jurisdiction over the contract if an issue was to arise.

Furthermore, if you were entering a contract with someone who resided in a different state and they decided to sue you, saying that you breached the agreement, would you want to travel to that state to defend the alleged claims because you chose that jurisdiction for your contract deal? Maybe not.

CHOICE OF LAW

When I tell you no one - I mean **no one** - that I've ever advised or who has come into my office seeking contractual representation have presented a contract with a choice of law provision.

Choice of law is amazing because it allows the parties to choose which state's law they want to apply to the contract in the event of a dispute (i.e. trial). This provision, along with the Jurisdiction provision, allows you to choose state law that may be more favorable if things were to get fired up between you and the opposing party.

This is something that you should always keep in mind especially if you are making a deal with someone in another state, because possibly your state has more favorable rules.

ATTORNEY FEES & COST

Generally, contracts that do not provide for attorney fees and cost cannot be requested for unless there's a statute that provides for these sorts of damages.

Why? One of the most basic principles of contract law is the measure of damages. By law, when the opposing party fails to abide by contract and causes you damages because of their failure, you're only entitled to what you would have received had the other party performed as agreed. Without this attorney fee provision, you will have left yourself vulnerable to the whim of some "hopeful" statute to provide you with these damages.

Outside of attorney fees, you want to contract for any special, incidental, and consequential damages that can be foreseen at the time of contracting. What are these?

Special Damages: are specific damages that flow to the injured party as a direct result of the breach.

Consequential damages: are indirect damages that are acquired at the end of the breach.

Incidental damages: are those costs or damages that you suffered as a direct result of the other party's breach.

And Cost: You always want to ensure that the other party (or the winning party) will agree to pay for costs associated with bringing a case.

Although every state is different in terms of how it applies rules for damages in breach of contract cases, it's always necessary that you spell out all possible damages and argue its reasonableness later.

DISPUTE RESOLUTION

People are often so happy at the outset of a new contractual relationship that they never stop to consider what happens if a dispute arises.

This is a golden opportunity to discuss how the parties will deal with disputes when they arise. Typically dispute provisions can be written all sorts of ways detailing how and when to submit a disputable issue for review, including whether one party will limit the other's ability to bring suit in a court of law and more.

For example, some provisions – especially if the contracting parties were long-time friends – may only agree that if a dispute arises between them that they will submit the issue to a neutral third-party for decision (i.e. a mediator). If one party does not like the decision, then the parties can submit the dispute to Arbitration. Oftentimes, long-time friendships and family members may agree to make arbitration binding.

If arbitration is binding, generally that means that the losing party will be bound by the terms of the arbitration award and foreclosed to seeking a different decision by filing a claim in court.

Let me back up for a moment so you can understand these terms. *Mediation* is the process whereby parties can submit a dispute to a third-party who is unbiased to help the parties sort through their differences and come to an agreement. This process is very informal and the parties can agree to have a decision be binding or non-binding at this stage. Most people do not.

Arbitration, on the other hand, is like a mini trial. The difference is that the rules of evidence – something lawyers must follow in court – is very relaxed. This process is designed to allow the aggrieved party to have their claim heard but is more streamlined and less expensive than taking a claim up the channels through an initial filing to trial to be heard.

Often, the arbitrating parties represent themselves, but they are not foreclosed from hiring legal representation to assist them along the way.

You should never get caught up in the "moment of getting the deal" and just sign the agreement without giving these things some thought. You should always look to see if there's a dispute resolution, as it can help to avoid being blindsided with a lawsuit if the other party is claiming you're at fault for some reason or another.

READ THE CONTRACT!

Although this portion is simply a reminder - a theoretical thump on the forehead – and not a provision, you must know and understand what's in your contract. You must know what you are getting and what you are giving. There's simply no excuse for laziness when it comes to this.

Remember, there are other provisions that will be necessary to ensure an air-tight agreement depending on the scope of the agreement, the objective of the parties, the type of industry you're involved with, and so on. However, these contractual provisions are provided to give you a snapshot idea of what most definitely should be present before signing. Always consult with a lawyer to ensure your rights are protected.

"Reading is important, because if you can read, you can learn anything about everything and everything about anything."

~

Tomie dePaola

CHAPTER 14

Team Curation for Sustainable Success

Do you know folks who are "do it yourselfers" and defy the need of having a team? I do. There are thousands, if not millions, of entrepreneurs and small business owners who refuse to build a team around their business or brand.

When this happens, there's only so far you can go because you're only one person. There's only so much one person can do and handle. Anything outside of that is just pure chaos and stressful. I have been there, and not because I didn't want a team, I just didn't know how to build a team or what I even needed a team for. But you live and you learn.

I always knew that I wanted to own my own law firm but never really thought about how that firm would look. What key players would I have and what would be their essential functions. And let me be honest, there are many other entrepreneurs and small business owners out there who had the same thought patterns and struggles to build something solid. That's because we all have failed – at one point or another – to think backwards.

What do I mean by that? If I would have thought about where my hypothetical law firm would be (in terms of success) around the fifth- or seventh-year mark, I could have begun the process of thinking retroactively to what I would need at every stage to achieve those goals. But, like many… I didn't.

I want to help you avoid making the same mistake. It took me longer to get this piece, but now that I know what to do, I'm passing the knowledge on to you.

In my book, *What Are You Sporting About?*©, I discuss the different foundations that businesses need for success. Those foundations include the following: legal, financial, insurance, tax, qualified mentor, and therapist. Since we're dealing with sports and potential endorsements, I'll add another one – sports agent.

We will be breaking these foundations down so that you can get a sense of the key players you need to make your new entrepreneurial journey work.

LEGAL REPRESENTATIVE

I always lead with legal representation because that's what I do. But all jokes aside, it's very necessary and frequently undervalued. As you now know from reading this book, having legal representation is paramount – not only to your success as an entrepreneur – but the survival of your brand.

Lawyers can provide instrumental and strategic support at every stage of the process from initial communications regarding terms of a potential agreement, to the negotiation table, to signing the agreement, to litigating the matter (to prosecute or defend) if necessary, in case of a violation plus more.

Although historically lawyers have been considered extremely expensive, attorneys are catching on that many people cannot afford a high billable rate. Thus, many are creating plans and other charging formats to support those in need by also helping the client to afford the representation.

Take my firm for instance - we provide legal plans that are built around the peculiar needs of the client. There's a monthly flat fee that is paid (if ongoing representation) or a contingency fee if it's simply based on an endorsement or sponsorship deal of some kind.

This way, there's no surprises to the client, the client understands what comes next, they are more prepared to plan their business's finances for the year.

FINANCIAL REPRESENTATIVE

Financial advisors have gotten a bad reputation, especially among the sporting community because many have taken advantage of their athlete clients. However, that doesn't mean that you should forego choosing a financial representative. Furthermore, this is all the reason to keep watch over your finances, ask questions and check in regularly to understand and ensure the proper safeguarding of your assets.

As for my student athletes, if you look at the name, image, and likeness legislation of most states that have passed their bills, they talk about having a financial representative and lawyer. You should take that as an "Aha" moment to understand that if legislatures have made it a point to discuss this, then maybe you do need them on your team.

As you start to gear up to profit from your name, image, or likeness, you need someone who can help you manage your funds. A financial advisor can help you set up a retirement or some other savings fund, look into insurance plans that may build equity later and connect you with other key players that will be necessary for your entrepreneurial success.

A financial advisor will also help you to budget appropriately so you can avoid "robbing Peter to pay Paul" scenario as you've most likely seen other people do.

You don't want to have plans for your money before you even get it. You know what I mean? Like, I know you know someone either in your family or a friend who has so much liability and debt that before they even collect their paycheck, it's already accounted for. That's a sad life to live. It's stressful, its overwhelming, it's suffocating, and it's limiting.

Your financial advisor will help you to craft plans to pay down debt (if you have it), by also creating a mechanism to build wealth.

INSURANCE REPRESENTATIVE

Now, you are an athlete so this should be a no-brainer. If the only reason a person wants to do business with you (let's say a sports sponsor) because you have a mean right arm as a pitcher and they pay you per strike outs, it may be a great idea to insure your arm in the event of an injury.

Think about it, in that scenario, your pitching ability is the very thing that helps you to get paid. Thus, if you're no longer able to pitch for purposes of receiving payment from the sports sponsor, you want to be compensated.

Insurance is another undervalued asset that many people don't want to spend money on. However, insurance is also one of the fastest mechanisms to wealth. This is one reason why the rich stay rich. If they lose something, they don't get frantic because it was insured! They cash in!

TAX REPRESENTATIVE

Now, if you are receiving profit from your name, image, and likeness, you're in business. In Chapter 11, *Safeguarding Your ASSets*, I discuss a few common business entity structures because you'll need a mechanism to avoid the grappling tax liability that will come your way.

If you're a student athlete, you've probably been chilling out by allowing your parents to claim you on their taxes. If you are a professional athlete, you're probably discovering how exhausting and expensive taxes are. The game is going to change when you become a business. Meaning, you are filing and registering a business entity in your name and have those checks cut to the business for tax purposes. A tax representative will help guide you in determining how much liability you owe and how much you can save.

If you are lazy and fail to file that business although you're making a considerable amount of coin, you'll be making the worst decision to operate as a sole proprietorship because you'll be taxed 100% on all the income you receive with no business deduction benefits.

QUALIFIED MENTOR

You will need someone to tell you "like it is," champion you on, strategize with you, be your confidante, etc. This could be one person or many. What I've known to be true is that qualified mentors will aide you at every level of your success by giving you real advice and helping you through the tough hurdles.

It's important, however, to refrain from putting people in this position who are not qualified and are simply offering their feelings as opposed to true facts or strategy that will help you succeed.

Be mindful that a spiritual advisor can also be a qualified mentor. Your athletic coach, a teacher, a relative can all be qualified mentors. You will have to implement discernment over what value each person brings and why they are necessary to your achievement.

Let me give you an example. One of my qualified mentors is another notable attorney here in the Chicagoland area. We were having a conversation about this large company coming on as a client and I said something to the effect, "I'll need to hire someone to teach me things about that industry." He stopped me there and said the following:

> No. You stop saying that right now. YOU ARE THE LAWYER. And there's no-one who can teach you how to do what you do. An industry is an industry. A contract is a contract is a contract no matter how you look at it and you're already an expert on that. You take the time you need, read it, and read it some more. But you never say that again because you already have everything you need.

Immediately, I said to him, "Thank you. I didn't realize what I was saying was so limiting until you interrupted me and blasted it in my face."

This is what I mean. My mentor is the bomb and he challenges me to think differently and better each and every time we speak.

THERAPIST

Having a therapist has been extremely stigmatized. Honestly, there's nothing wrong with having a trained medical professional to help you sort out your feelings, problems, and chaotic life.

People have increasingly jumped on the bandwagon of "stay strong," or "you'll get through this." Sometimes, you might not. It's time to stop thinking that you're built to carry the weight of the world on your shoulders.

And I'm getting real with you right now, *spiritually*, because I don't believe that God would want you to burden yourself that way either! Different people were given different gifts to help others in need. There's a gift that you embody that will - or has - touched a life. A therapist can do the same for you. We all have had some type of mental health hurdle that we have to overcome.

Let's face it, if you're black and brown, you're more likely dealing with more trauma than the average person for reasons I don't need to list here. If you're a member of the LGBTQA+ community, you probably are also. We all are.

My point is: don't underestimate the power of a therapist to help you sort through your issues. You're not "less-than" because you need help. Seeking helps shows strength and commitment to self! It will help you to get clear about where you are, what you want, and where you want to go. Anyone who can do that should be given a trophy!

SPORTS AGENT/ATHLETE ADVISOR

We already know that professional athletes have sprots agents to help them get deals, or market them to teams for purposes of being drafted. But what about student athletes.

Well, as you know student athletes weren't allowed to speak with third parties around deals related to their name, image, and likeness, and therefore, never really had agents.

I think this team member is very important for student athletes to know because the new NIL rules are stating that student athletes should have athlete advisors and/or agents.

Whether you're trying to wrap your head around team creation as student athlete or pro, athlete advisors (sports agents) can help you navigate sponsorship and endorsement deals. The agent can also shop you around to pro teams. This will help to get you ahead of the curve. But, like anyone else, you must stay in touch with your advisor and ensure that they have your best interest in mind.

Although it is possible to run a business without a team, it's extremely hectic. There are too many blind spots that you are not equipped to navigate. You will need additional people to help you realize the next phase of success that you're dreaming about. For now, start with the foundational key players that will help you get started and create a roadmap so you know where you're going and what to expect.

> *"Coming together is a beginning. Keeping together is progress. Working together is success."*
>
> ~
>
> ***Henry Ford***

Estate Planning.
Yes, You Need It!

You know the saddest thing I've found is the enormous number of people who do not have an estate plan of any sorts! Estate planning is not just creating a Last Will & Testament, it's ensuring that you organize your assets, create strategic plans to protect the assets, and also put measures in place to keep your enterprise operating and generating revenue if you were to become seriously ill, disabled, or worse.

As you create new brands around your name, image, and likeness, you're establishing an estate with assets. It doesn't make sense to leave those things unprotected.

Here's a story for you on why estate planning is imperative. Buckle up! A woman - also a drug addict – was married for about 12 years. She was estranged from her husband (how long, I'm not sure), but the two had a daughter who was handicapped. The woman's mother arranged for life insurance for her because she knew that something would possibly happen to the woman considering the lifestyle she was living.

The woman's mother died; subsequently, the woman's sister and father continued paying on the insurance policy. Years go by and the woman and her estranged husband have never filed for divorce. The drug addicted woman passes away. (From what, I don't know). The woman leaves behind a minor daughter. It turns out that the policy the mother got on her daughter was a $50,000.00 death insurance plan.

The woman never had an estate plan (or Will), the woman's mother only listed herself as the beneficiary on the policy. Since the woman's husband was still living, the issue became whether the woman's husband was entitled to 100% of the insurance proceeds, where the husband could take 50% of the distribution with the other 50% going to the daughter, or whether the family could argue that the daughter (of the drug addicted woman) should have 100% of the proceeds since the husband had been estranged for over 10 years from the woman.

I mean – GOOD LORD, what a situation! And this really is a true story! Most people don't create estate plans because they think they don't have anything. What you must be cognizant of is that, if you don't create a plan detailing how you want your estate disbursed, the state will do that for you. In that instance, this means potentially allowing people who have no relationship with you to take part in your estate after your death.

Think about this; depending on the State that you live in, if you passed away unmarried, no children and no estate plan in place, your estate would be divided between your parents. Now, what if you've been estranged from one of your parents for years?

Let's go a step further. Let's say both parents were deceased, but you have siblings, a few with whom you've never had a good relationship. Suppose that maybe one sibling is a half sibling that you don't know much about.

Guess what, if your parents are deceased and you didn't have children or a spouse, your estate assets would be split among the siblings you leave behind regardless of the relationship you had or didn't have.

Therefore, estate planning is particularly important, and you should start implementing it now!

POWER OF ATTORNEY

Here are a few things you can start doing to implement an estate plan. Have an attorney draft a Power of Attorney (POA) document for you. Most states do have a standard POA document, however, if you go that route, ensure that everything you need covered is listed properly.

A **POA** gives a person or persons authorization to act on your behalf when you are unable to. This could be while you are temporarily away, severally ill, or incapacitated. You can control the length of time you want a person(s) to act in this role, and the substance of what the person(s) would be responsible to do.

Through a POA, you can authorize folks to control your financial accounts, any real estate, personal property, and more. You may also appoint a person(s) to make medical decisions for you. It all depends on you and your needs.

For instance, a *Durable POA* allows the person you appoint to handle your affairs even after you fall ill. Most importantly, it takes effect right after it's signed. A *non-durable POA*, ends when you become incapacitated or die and will remove any previous appointed responsibilities.

A *medical POA* (aka medical directive) appoints a person to make medical decisions on your behalf in the event you are medically determined incapable of making such decisions. This type of POA becomes effective right after it's signed.

You could also grant someone *"Special"* or *Limited POA*. This means that you appoint someone to do one specific thing for you. It could be a few things. However, once the tasks appointed are completed, that POA is concluded. For example, if you appointed a person Limited POA for purposes of paying an electric bill or renewing an agreement for you, that Limited POA will expire once the given task is completed or upon a specified date that you dictate in the agreement.

It's also possible to have multiple agents who act on your behalf with different types of POAs. For example, you can have more than one Limited POA to ensure a form of "check and balance" on your assets.

The Last type of POA is a *springing POA*. This is a type of conditional POA. This POA will take effect upon a certain event that you specify taking place for the appointed agent to act. For example, if you were drafted into a Euro Pro League and had to leave immediately to play overseas, you could have a springing POA that appoints someone to take care of any financial needs so that your transition is smooth.

Even if you have a POA, you still need a Will (and possibly a trust) to provide protection and additional direction on how you'd like your assets to be divided or handled.

WILLS & TRUSTS

You're probably saying, "Sivonnia is crazy. Why in the heck is she talking about a Will? I'm not old." Look. Do you know how many young people die every day? Some were phenomenal people that never took the time to think about who they wanted to take care of after death. Don't think of this as a debilitating task, but think of it as something that will allow your soul to rest freely when you're gone.

Now, there are two types of Wills that I want you to be cognizant about: A **Living Will** and a **Last Will & Testament**.

A *Last Will & Testament* is the most popular since most people know that their grandparents most likely have one in place. This sort of Will provides for how the deceased person wants their property divided and names an "executor" or "administrator" to execute the terms of the will.

A *Living Will*, by contrast, is a directive in the event of some medical happening where you lay out your wishes and decisions for medications, surgical procedures, etc. You may be thinking that the Medical POA will take care of this? No, it does not! Unlike the Medical POA, you would be the one making the determination in a Living Will about what decisions you want to be made related to your medical care. In the POA, you appoint someone else to make those decisions for you.

Now, a **Living Trust** is an actual trust where you transfer assets for the benefit of people that you name as beneficiaries under the trust. When you create a Trust, you must name a Trustee who's basically the steward of the trust and who will be responsible for transferring the assets to the beneficiaries upon your death.

Many people think that creating a Last Will & Testament will keep their estate from going through *Probate* (the vehicle to litigate claims related to the will and heirs), but having a Trust shields your assets from being part of a lengthy and costly court battle.

My point: take heed to the information here, seek advice from a knowledgeable and trustworthy Trust & Estate Lawyer because when you think about Protecting your Name, Image, & Likeness, it goes beyond what you see and do today! It's much deeper than that.

"Estate Planning is an important and everlasting gift you can give your family."
~
Suze Orman

CHAPTER 16

The Conclusion

Congratulations! You've gotten through all of my lessons, chastisements, legal mumbo jumbo and more. The fact that you've made it to the end of the book speaks volumes on your willingness to be challenged outside your norm and comfort zone.

I want you to remember that regardless of your athletic level, collegiate, professional or retired, you still have a name, image, and likeness that deserves protection. Never allow people to walk over you. Never allow people to treat you like you're inferior to them because of the degrees they may carry. You're just as capable of understanding and educating yourself to make the right decisions.

Whatever you decide to do with your name, image, and likeness is your decision but you must be a diligent steward over it to ensure it remains protected.

Check out the resources in the back of this book I've compiled to help you get started. Check out my free podcast – *What Are You Sporting About?* - to listen to amazing stories and strides by athletes and those connected to sports. Follow the IG and FB pages @whatareyousportingabout and @athletesmakingmoves for additional content, motivation, and education.

Business & Legal Consulting. If you are looking for me to support you individually by strategizing, creating accountability, and implementing safeguards for your success, go over to www.sldebarros.com to learn more about the services I provide.

Legal Support. If you need legal advice and representation in all things business and sports, make sure you visit www.sldebarros.com or follow me on social at @sldebarroslaw. I'm here to help and protect you. That's why they call me the Protector of Athletes™.

Speaking. If you would like for me to speak to your group about sports, business, entrepreneurship, business, or sports law, visit www.prosportlawyer.com.

Online *Athletes Making Moves* **Shop**. In my online shop, we offer tons of fun and inspirational apparel, books, stickers and more to keep you making moves. Shop now at www.athletesmakingmoves.com

Athletes Making Moves **Mastermind**. This is for my athletes who want to dive deeper into the business aspects that will create the framework for a greater return in the future. Members of the mastermind will have an opportunity to meet with me 1-on-1, enjoy access to fun live events, receive more hands-on support to ensure that you're making the right moves. If you'd like to learn more, visit athletesmakingmoves.com.

You can also find me online through your favorite social media platform at:

FIRM		SPORTS
Twitter:	@ SLDeBarros_Law	
Facebook:	@SLDeBarrosLaw	@whatareyousportingabout
Instagram:	@SLDeBarrosLaw	@athletesmakingmoves
LinkedIn:	@sldebarroslaw	

And lastly, you're not alone so don't act like you are. Build the team you need. Take the time to vet people. Follow your gut – your initial thoughts and you'll make the right decision, because like Les says …

"It's not over until you win."
~ Les Brown

ABOUT THE AUTHOR

Sivonnia DeBarros - Protector of Athletes™ - is a first-generation lawyer and law business owner, and a former track and field Division-I College athlete. DeBarros graduated from Chicago-Kent College of Law with her J.D. in 2013, received a M.S. in Criminal Justice from Everest University in 2010, and her B.S. in Political Science from University of South Florida in 2008.

DeBarros has represented pro athletes from the NFL, MLS, NBA-G League, and Pro-Table Tennis sports. She's also represented 7- figure National Brands and NY Times Best-Selling Authors by helping them to properly set up businesses, put proper agreements in place and create legacies that will pay dividends in the future.

DeBarros has been featured on platforms like CBS Chicago, ABC Channel 7, WGN, & Shoutout LA; including a host of podcast platforms where she exhibits her passion for athletes, women, and first-generation business owners earning the name – *Protector of Athletes.*

Additionally, DeBarros is a public speaker, entrepreneur, and the bestselling author of *What Are You Sporting About?* DeBarros is the creator of the proprietary program "Have Your S.A.E.™" that was designed with college athletes in mind and the author of, Athletes Making Moves©, releasing July 31, 2021.

DeBarros previously authored *The Foreign Sovereign Immunities Act: The Roadblocks to Recovery* law article, published in Chicago-Kent College Of Law's Seventh Circuit's Review Law Journal, and published the new Children's Books, JoJo Learns About Credibility and JoJo Learns About Voting, which are the first two books of her new Children Series, *JoJo's Legal Adventures* that can be purchased at www.jjlegaladventures.com

Learn more about Attorney DeBarros, her firm or her publications by visiting www.sldebarros.com.

You can purchase the book - What Are You Sporting About? or listen to the podcast at www.prosportlawyer.com.

To purchase Athletes Making Moves or to shop, visit www.athletesmakingmoves.com.

ATHLETE
ENTREPRENEUR
RESOURCES

PODCAST

Access episodes each week on all platforms where podcasts can be found.

Get this book at www.prosportlawyer.com

STUDENT ATHLETE AUDIT

Who's Your Support (25pts)

0-No confidence	1-aware/no confidence	2-emerging confidence	3-some confidence	4-Mostly Confident	5-Extremely Confident
Parent(s)/Legal Guardian(s)	-	-	-	-	-
Coach(es)	-	-	-	-	-
Teammate(s)	-	-	-	-	-
Professor(s)	-	-	-	-	-
Significant Other	-	-	-	-	-
Others?	-	-	-	-	-

Who's On Your Team (25pts)

Category	0- /no confidence	1-aware/no confidence	2-emerging confidence	3-some confidence	4-Mostly Confident	5-Extremely Confident
Insurance Agent(s)	-	-	-	-	-	-
Financial/CPA(s)	-	-	-	-	-	-
Attorney(s)	-	-	-	-	-	-
Mentor(s)	-	-	-	-	-	-
Therapist(s)	-	-	-	-	-	-
Others?	-	-	-	-	-	-

Tell Us About Your Career (25pts)

Category	0- /no confidence	1-aware/no confidence	2-emerging confidence	3-some confidence	4-Mostly Confident	5-Extremely Confident
Career Counselor(s)	-	-	-	-	-	-
Have a Resume?	-	-	-	-	-	-

Have a Cover Letter?	-	-	-	-	-	-
Work Experience?	-	-	-	-	-	-
Plans Post Sports?	-	-	-	-	-	-

Name, Image and Likeness (25pts)

Category	0- /no confidence	1- aware/no confidence	2-emerging confidence	3-some confidence	4-Mostly Confident	5- Extremely Confident
Do you understand the NIL Rules?	-	-	-	-	-	-
Have you discussed the rules with a parent/legal guardian?	-	-	-	-	-	-
Do you understand the legal implications?	-	-	-	-	-	-
Understand how sponsorships and endorsements work?	-	-	-	-	-	-
Do you understand what a "conflict of issue" is?	-	-	-	-	-	-

Current Business Assets? (25pts)

Category	0- /no confidence	1- aware/no confidence	2- emerging confidence	3-some confidence	4-Mostly Confident	5- Extremely Confident
Do you own a trademark?	-	-	-	-	-	-
Do you own a copyright?	-	-	-	-	-	-
Have a registered business?	-	-	-	-	-	-
Pay taxes?	-	-	-	-	-	-
Have a sponsorship or endorsement deal?	-	-	-	-	-	-

Your S.A.E. Confidence? (25pts)

Category	0- /no confidence	1- aware/no confidence	2- emerging confidence	3-some confidence	4-Mostly Confident	5- Extremely Confident

Have Difficulty Answering Questions?	-	-	-	-	-	-
Do you have challenges you feel will keep you from success?	-	-	-	-	-	-
Live with anxiety or fear?	-	-	-	-	-	-
Do you have short-term and long-term goals?	-	-	-	-	-	-
Are you proud of yourself?	-	-	-	-	-	-

Input all scores for each category to see how you scored.

SCORING:	Your Support	Your Team	Career	NIL	Assets	Confidence
Enter Total Score Here: _____/100						

PRO ATHLETE AUDIT

Who's On Your Team (25pts)

Category	0- /no confidence	1-aware/no confidence	2-emerging confidence	3-some confidence	4-Mostly Confident	5- Extremely Confident
Insurance Agent(s)	-	-	-	-	-	-
Financial/CPA(s)	-	-	-	-	-	-
Attorney(s)	-	-	-	-	-	-
Mentor(s)	-	-	-	-	-	-
Therapist(s)/Counselor	-	-	-	-	-	-
Others?	-	-	-	-	-	-

Tell Us About Your Career Experience (25pts)

Category	0- /no confidence	1-aware/no confidence	2-emerging confidence	3-some confidence	4-Mostly Confident	5- Extremely Confident
I have Career/Life Coach.	-	-	-	-	-	-
I've been employed for the last 2 years.	-	-	-	-	-	-
My job is fulfilling.	-	-	-	-	-	-
I have a college degree or higher.	-	-	-	-	-	-
I am a self-proclaimed entrepreneur.	-	-	-	-	-	-

Networking Experience (25pts)

Category	0- /no confidence	1-aware/no confidence	2-emerging confidence	3-some confidence	4-Mostly Confident	5- Extremely Confident
I have been recruited (sports & otherwise)	-	-	-	-	-	-
I've cold-emailed someone	-	-	-	-	-	-

I have Connection with other business owners	-	-	-	-	-
I have Connections with other athletes in business	-	-	-	-	-
I have cultivated relationship from these connections	-	-	-	-	-

Name, Image and Likeness (25pts)

Category	0- /no confidence	1-aware/no confidence	2-emerging confidence	3-some confidence	4-Mostly Confident	5-Extremely Confident
I understand NIL as it relates to my status.	-	-	-	-	-	-
NIL applies to pro and retired athletes.	-	-	-	-	-	-
NIL is an intellectual property right.	-	-	-	-	-	-
I understand NIL's legal implications.	-	-	-	-	-	-
I understand what a right of publicity is.	-	-	-	-	-	-

Your Business Assets? (25pts)

Category	0- /no confidence	1-aware/no confidence	2-emerging confidence	3-some confidence	4-Mostly Confident	5-Extremely Confident
I have a registered business	-	-	-	-	-	-
I have a copyright	-	-	-	-	-	-
I have a trademark	-	-	-	-	-	-
I have pitched to a sponsor	-	-	-	-	-	-
I have received a sponsorship or endorsement deal before	-	-	-	-	-	-

Let's Test Your Confidence (25pts)

Category	0- /no confidence	1- aware/no confidence	2- emerging confidence	3-some confidence	4-Mostly Confident	5- Extremely Confident
I have found your purpose in life	-	-	-	-	-	-
I have challenges that will keep you from success	-	-	-	-	-	-
I live with anxieties or fears	-	-	-	-	-	-
I have both short-term and long-term goals	-	-	-	-	-	-
Sports is my identity	-	-	-	-	-	-

Input all scores for each category to see how you scored.

SCORING:	Your Support	Your Team	Career	NIL	Assets	Confidence
Enter Total Score Here: _____/150						

Test Your Confidence & Identity

To know what you want out of life, you must know who you are and what steps you need to take to build confidence to go after it.

General Questions for College & Pro-Athletes:

1. How would you explain your identity? How does sports play a role in your identity?

_____

_____

_____

_____

_____

2. What is your proudest accomplishment? Why?

I ask this question because it's imperative that you celebrate your achievements. Celebration builds confidence. Confidence welcome opportunities.

_____

_____

_____

_____

_____

_____

3. What are your short-term goals (think academically, athletically, personally, and professionally)?

_____

_____

_____

_____

_____

_____

4. What are your long-term goals (going professional? sponsorships? financial stability? Business ownership)?

_____

_____

_____

_____

_____

5. What do you perceive as barriers toward achieving these goals?

_____

_____

_____

_____

6. What are your current fears, uncertainties, and questions?

_____

_____

_____

_____

_____

_____

7. <u>Congratulations</u>! You have confronted yourself with some hard stuff. So let's flip the script and pull out all of the positive things that you've said about yourself:

My Identity is: _____

My Short-term goal is: _____
because I want/need to do _____

My long-term goal is: _____
because I want/need to do _____

I'm willing to work towards doing _____
to remove the barriers that I perceive are getting in the way.

I am NOT afraid of _____ because I know I hold the power and key to my future.

<u>Remember</u>: There is power in the mind and the tongue. You must speak those things as though they were and also put action behind them. I not too long ago said to a colleague that I believe "I operate scared all the time." Meaning that there's much that frightens me but I would remain stuck and unable to pour into others if I didn't get up and MOVE in spite of how scary and uncertain it feels.

That's life! Scary. Uncertain. Unchartered at times. But it's also rewarding, exhilarating and peaceful. Your future is what you make it.

NIL: Negotiation & Contract Tracker

Sport: _____

School Name: _____

SAE Name: _____

Date:	Company/Br and Name	Type of Proposal Made	Expected Compensation/ Arrangement	Contract Finalized Y/N	Disclosure Made to School/Date/School Official contacted.	Format Disclosure Made	Response provided/Appro val & Date Made

LEGAL
Issue Tracker
Copy and Re-use for each issue.

Date:	List the Issue:	Statement or Action Made?	To whom was it made?	Who did what?
	Y/N	Reported to who? →		
Matter Reported?		By what Method?		
Witnesses:	Y/N	Names	Address	Ph/Email
Recourse Taken?	Y/N	By Who?	Title	Ph/Email

Know Your TEAM

Name: _____ Year _____

Brand Name: _____

Team Member:	Type/Agency:	Address:	Ph#:	Fax:	Email:	Addt'l Info:
Lawyer	Practice Area:					Business Sports & Entertainment Family Real Estate Estate & Trusts Securities (i.e. Stocks) Criminal Defense
SPORTS AGENT:	Agency's Name				:	**Assistant?**
ADVISORY REP: Name:	Agency?					**Advising on What?**
INSURANCE REP: Name:	Agency Name:					**Insured What?** **Premium$:** _____ **What's Insured?**
FINANCIAL ADVISOR Name:						**How does agent get paid?** **Self-Educational Materials Reviewed?** _____
Qualified Mentor(s) Name(s)	Type of Mentor:	Address:	Ph#	Fax#	Email:	Additional Info:

CPA/Accountant **CPA:** **Accountant:**					
Other Team Member:					

Always review your relationship and team dynamics and update this annually.

Quick Guide to Legal Business Entities

Business Entity Type	Registered Agent to File	Recognized in Each State?	Is this a tax election?	Taxed Twice?
LLC – Limited Liability Company	✔	✔	-	✔
PLLC – Professional Limited Liability Company	✔	No	-	No Will pass through to the individual members if more than one partner
Corporation (c-Corp)	✔	✔	-	YES & NO ✔ The Corp. pays taxes on its earnings and does not distribute to individual partners. Partners are only taxed as an employee or through corporate dividends as shareholders with a lower tax rate.
S – Corporation	✔	✔	✔	✔ But, can also pay its shareholder dividends which are taxed at a lower rate.
General Partnership	✔	✔	-	✔
LLP – Limited Liability Partnership	✔	No	-	✔
PC – Professional Corporation	✔	✔	-	✔

END NOTES

1 Summary of NCAA Regulations, Division One, Academic Yr. 2011-2012, http://fs.ncaa.org/Docs/AMA/compliance_forms/DI/DI%20Summary%20of%20NCAA%20Regulations.pdf

2 *Id.* See NCAA Bylaw 12.3.1

3 Soraya McDonald, *HBO's 'The Scheme' feels like a commercial for Christian Dawkins, and not much else,* March 31, 2020, https://theundefeated.com/features/hbos-the-scheme-feels-like-a-commercial-for-christian-dawkins-and-not-much-else/

4 *Id.*

5 Jeff Borzello and Mark Schlabach, *Dawkins, Code convicted in college hoops trial,* May 8, 2019, https://www.espn.com/mens-college-basketball/story/_/id/26701792/dawkins-code-convicted-college-hoops-trial

6 The United States Department of Justice - Southern District of New York, *U.S. Attorney Announces The Arrest Of 10 Individuals, Including Four Division I Coaches, For College Basketball Fraud And Corruption Schemes,* September 26, 2017, https://www.justice.gov/usao-sdny/pr/us-attorney-announces-arrest-10-individuals-including-four-division-i-coaches-college

7 *Id.,* see also Borzello and Schlabach, En.62

8 *Id.* at Borzello and Schlabach, *Dawkins, Code convicted in college hoops trial.*

9 Mirin Fader, *BRIBERY SCANDAL NIGHTMARE: Brian Bowen was a 5-star recruit and future lottery pick. Tony Bland was a star recruiter on the head coaching fast track. Then the FBI came knocking. A few years later, they're still picking up the pieces,* May 13, 2019, https://bleacherreport.com/articles/2835899-brian-bowen-left-in-the-wake-of-the-ncaa-bribery-scandal-nightmare

10 *Id.*

11 ESPN.com, *Lawyer says family hasn't repayed rent, other cash,* April 28, 2006, https://www.espn.com/college-football/news/story?id=2425136

12 Dennis Dodd, *30 years later: The legacy of SMU's death penalty and six teams nearly hit with one,* February 22, 2017, https://www.cbssports.com/college-football/news/30-years-later-the-legacy-of-smus-death-penalty-and-six-teams-nearly-hit-with-one/

13 *Id.*

14 Paul Myerberg, *National College Players Association asks Congress to pursue broad-based reform' in adopting compensation for student-athletes,* June 25, 2020, https://www.usatoday.com/story/sports/college/2020/06/25/national-college-players-association-asks-congress-reform/3254952001/

15 *Id.*

16 *Id.*

17 Ross Dellenger, *NCAA Presents Congress With Bold Proposal for NIL Legislation,* July 31, 2020, https://www.si.com/college/2020/07/31/ncaa-

sends-congress-nil-legislation-
proposal#&gid=ci026b661b40002686&pid=ncaa-nil-draft-language--3

[18] *SAE, The Acronym for Student-Athlete Entrepreneur,* and used creatively for literary thought, expression and impact.

[19] California Legislative SB206, Chapter 383, Fair Play to Play Act, Oct. 1, 2019,
https://leginfo.legislature.ca.gov/faces/billTextClient.xhtml?bill_id=2019 20200SB206

[20] Florida State Senate, *Student Athlete Achievement Act,* SB656, Chapter 2020-28, 1004.098, Sec. 2, June 12, 2020,
https://www.flsenate.gov/Session/Bill/2020/646

[21] Florida's Age of majority
https://www.flsenate.gov/Laws/Statutes/2012/Chapter743/All

[22] *Id.* at Sec. 2.; 1004.098, Sec. 6.

[23] *Id.* at Sec. (5)(b)

[24] *Id.* at Sec. (5)(a)(1) and (2)

[25] *Id.* at (5)(b)

[26] D'Onofrio, Jessica and Wall, Craig, Gov. *Pritzker signs Illinois student-athlete compensation bill at U of I,* June 29, 2021, https://abc7chicago.com/gov-jb-pritzker-university-of-illinois-student-athlete-compensation-bill-college-athlete/10842867/

[27] Illinois Student Endorsement Act, (*Proposed Legislation*) SB2338, Section 5.

[28] *Id.*

[29] *Id.*

[30] *Id.* at Sec. 10(2)

[31] IL Student Endorsement Act at 20(h)

[32] *Id.*

[33] *Id.* at Sec. 25

[34] *Id.* at Sec. 20(c)

[35] *Id.*

[36] *Id.* at Sec. 15(f)

[37] Id. at 15(c)

[38] *Id.*

[39] *Id.*

[40] Florida Student-Athlete Achievement Act, SB646, S. 1004.098, (5)(a)(1).

[41] *Id.* at rule 1004.098, Section (1)(a)

[42] *Id.* at Section 5(b)

[43] *IL Student Endorsement Act* at Sec. 35.

[44] Sivonnia L. DeBarros, *What Are You Sporting About? For Aspiring, Current & Former Pro-Athletes in Business,* Chapter 7 – Know the Power of Your Legal Rights, pp. 57-58 (June 1, 2020).

[45] *Id.*

[46] *Id.*

47 ATHnet, *Sample Athletic Aid Agreement*, accessed on July 4, 2020 at https://www.athleticscholarships.net/wp-content/uploads/2013/01/Example-Athletic-Aid-Agreement.pdf

48 IL Student Endorsement Act at Sec. 35

49 *Hodges v. Buzzeo*, 193 F. Supp. 2d 1279, 1284 (M.D. Fla. 2002) (citing *Nautica Int'l. v. Intermarine USA, L.P.*, 5 F. Supp. 2d 1333, 1344 (S.D.Fla. 1998); *Salit v. Ruden, McClosky, Smith, Schuster & Russell, P.A.*, 742 So. 2d 381, 385 (Fla. 4th DCA 1999)).

50 IL Student Endorsement Act at Sec. 35.

51 Electronic Code of Federal Regulations, §86.31 Education Programs or Activities, accessed at https://www.ecfr.gov/cgi-bin/retrieveECFR?gp=&SID=d26dfaaeecd977dfa216731c71b060e0&mc=true&r=PART&n=pt45.1.86#se45.1.86_131

52 *Id.* at subsection (a)

53 *Id.* at subsection (b)

54 GA HB 617, 20-3-681(c)(4)(B)

55 *Id.* at (c)(4)(B)(i)

56 Barnaby Lane, *Michael Jordan's $2b Nike deal happened only thanks to his parents*, May 8, 2020, accessed at Financial Review Magazine, https://www.afr.com/companies/sport/michael-jordan-s-2b-nike-deal-happened-only-thanks-to-his-parents-20200508-p54r0r

57 *Id.*

58 *Id.*

59 *Id.*

60 Mike Ozanian, *Michael Jordan Sells Minority Interest In Hornets, And His Return Is Even Better Than Reports Suggest*, Sept. 20, 2019, (Forbes) accessed at https://www.forbes.com/sites/mikeozanian/2019/09/20/heres-michael-jordans-pretax-return-on-the-sale-of-the-charlotte-hornets/#7145847b31b6

61 *Id.*

62 *Id.*

63 Tadd Haislop, *Aaron Hernandez timeline: From murders and trials to prison suicide*, Jan 18, 2020, accessed at https://www.sportingnews.com/us/nfl/news/aaron-hernandez-timeline-murders-trials-prison-suicide/1886y82a8bgyx123qxcgg04lb5

64 Kevin Armstrong, *Hundreds of Patriots fans line up to exchange their Aaron Hernandez jerseys*, July 7, 2013, NY Daily News, accessed at https://www.nydailynews.com/sports/football/hundreds-line-exchange-aaron-hernandez-jerseys-article-1.1391723

65 Joseph Zucker, *NFL: Colin Kaepernick Has Raised Attention, Awareness on Social Justice Issues*, Sept. 4, 2018, https://bleacherreport.com/articles/2794156-nfl-colin-kaepernick-has-raised-attention-awareness-on-social-justice-issues

[66] *Id.*

[67] ABC News, *New Ray Rice Video Shows Moment He Punched Fiancée In Elevator,* https://abcnews.go.com/Sports/video/ray-rice-video-shows-moment-he-punched-fiancee-in-elevator-25349630

[68] Rachel Axon, *Ray Rice case prompted NFL changes on domestic violence, but cases continue to test policy,* Sept. 18, 2019, https://www.usatoday.com/story/news/investigations/2019/09/18/nfl-domestic-violence-ray-rice-tyreek-hill-ezekiel-elliott-adrian-peterson/2215187001/

[69] Aaron Wilson, *Financial ramifications of Ravens terminating Ray Rice's contract,* Sept. 8, 2014, https://www.baltimoresun.com/sports/ravens/bal-financial-ramifications-of-ravens-terminating-ray-rices-contract-20140908-story.html

[70] Jordan Ranaan, *Josh Brown on allegations of domestic violence: 'I never hit her',* Feb. 2, 2017, https://www.espn.com/nfl/story/_/id/18604215/former-new-york-giants-kicker-josh-brown-admits-domestic-violence-denies-hitting-wife

[71] *Id.*

[72] Soraya Roberts, *Chris Henry, Cincinnati Bengals star, 'aggravated' by wedding plans two days before death,* Dec. 18, 2009, accessed at https://www.nydailynews.com/entertainment/gossip/chris-henry-cincinnati-bengals-star-aggravated-wedding-plans-days-death-article-1.434015

[73] *Id.*

[74] *Id.*

[75] *Id.*

[76] A.J. Perez, *Ex-NFL player Rae Carruth released after nearly 19 years in prison for murder plot,* October 22, 2018, accessed at https://www.usatoday.com/story/sports/nfl/2018/10/22/rae-carruth-released-prison-panthers/1725206002/

[77] *Id.*

[78] *Id.*

[79] NBCS, *Jake Fromm called out by Oregon Ducks on discriminating text messages,* June 5, 2020, https://www.nbcsports.com/northwest/oregon-ducks/jake-fromm-called-out-oregon-ducks-discriminating-text-messages

[80] *Id.*

[81] Will Hobson, *Sylvia Hatchell accused of racially insensitive remarks, forcing UNC players to play hurt,* April 4, 2019, accessed at https://www.washingtonpost.com/sports/colleges/sylvia-hatchell-accused-of-racially-insensitive-remarks-forcing-unc-players-to-play-hurt/2019/04/04/499eb824-56f4-11e9-814f-e2f46684196e_story.html

[82] *Id.*

[83] *Id.*

[84] *Id.*

[85] John Branch, *Plaxico Burress accidentally Shoots Himself*, Nov. 29, 2008, https://www.nytimes.com/2008/11/30/sports/football/30burress.html#:~:text=Giants%20receiver%20Plaxico%20Burress%20accidentally,strain%20in%20the%20same%20leg.

[86] *Id.*

[87] John Clayton, *Burress' grievance nets $1M from Giants*, April 6, 2009, https://www.espn.com/nfl/news/story?id=4046141

[88] *Id.*

[89] Unknown Author, *Where did $312 million go? Boxing champ Evander Holyfield on his lost fortune*, Nov. 17, 2019, https://www.stuff.co.nz/sport/combat-sports/117488748/where-did-312-million-go-boxing-champ-evander-holyfield-on-his-lost-fortune#:~:text=Boxing%20champ%20Evander%20Holyfield%20on%20his%20lost%20fortune,-20%3A39%2C%20Nov&text=One%20of%20heavyweight%20boxing's%20biggest,26%20years%20in%20the%20ring.

[90] Michael McCain, *Kawhi Leonard Loses Copyright Lawsuit Against Nike Over Logo*, (April 23, 2020), Sports Illustrated, https://www.si.com/nba/2020/04/23/kawhi-leonard-loses-lawsuit-against-nike

[91] *Id.*

[92] *Id.*

[93] *Id.*

[94] *Id.*

[95] *Id.* (citing George Kiel III, *The Oral History of Kawhi Leonard's "Klaw" Logo*, (June 5, 2019), https://www.nicekicks.com/kawhi-leonard-says-claw-logo-idea/).

[96] Matthew Savare, *Publicity Rights: Image is everything.* (March 2013), Intellectual property magazine, accessed at www.intellectualpropertymagazine.com.

[97] California Legislature, *Right of Publicity, Penal Damages* §3344, at *https://leginfo.legislature.ca.gov/faces/codes_displaySection.xhtml?lawCode=CIV&sectionNum=3344.*

[98] Rightofpublicity.com, *Right of Publicity – Florida Statute* (*citing* FL ST §540.08. Unauthorized publication of name or likeness), accessed at https://rightofpublicity.com/statutes/florida